MW00624042

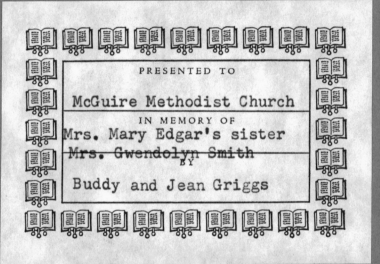

PRESENTED TO

McGuire Methodist Church

IN MEMORY OF

Mrs. Mary Edgar's sister

~~Mrs. Gwendolyn Smith~~

BY

Buddy and Jean Griggs

HEARTBEAT FOR GOD

Lee Etta Lappen is a staff member with Campus Crusade for Christ's Here's Life Ministries. As a campus staff member, she helped her husband, Elmer, direct both the Arizona area ministry and the campus ministry at Arizona State University for 23 years. She has three children, Jon, Beverly and Steve. A graduate of Bob Jones University, she frequently speaks at conferences and to women's groups.

Heartbeat for God

Lee Etta Lappen

with Maura Card

341

Here's Life Publishers, Inc.
P. O. Box 1576
San Bernardino, CA 92402

To my wonderful parents, Alfred and Eva Durham, who gave me my spiritual heritage and taught me to treasure the true riches in life.

Then I heard the voice of the Lord, saying, "Whom shall I send, and who will go for Us?" Then I said, "Here am I. Send me!"

— Isaiah 6:8

CONTENTS

FOREWORD

I first met Elmer and Lee Etta Lappen 24 short years ago when they were students. I was immediately struck by their unusual dedication to our Lord Jesus Christ. I cannot separate Lee Etta from Elmer because she cared for him in his deep pain, ministered together with him, prayed with him and encouraged him. Together they have been used of God to touch the lives of thousands of people, including my own.

Elmer's strong, determined, disciplined leadership in our Arizona ministry challenged students who were looking for something beyond mediocrity to join with him in his ministry for our Lord. Thousands came to Christ, and hundreds responded to his challenge to devote their lives to the Savior.

Crippled with arthritis, Elmer went through long years of therapy, discipline, hospitalization and constant pain. Yet through it all he trusted God. He continued to say and challenged others to say, "Lord, I will go. Send me."

Elmer echoed the words of the famous evangelist, Dwight L. Moody: "The world has yet to see what God can do through a man who is totally committed to Him. By the grace of God, I want to be that man."

My wife, Vonette, and I have always had a deep love and respect for Elmer and Lee Etta. During the 23 years that they have served on the Campus Crusade for Christ staff, they have been two of the most remarkable people I have ever known. Now Elmer has gone to be with the Lord, but Lee Etta continues to serve on our staff with special blessing.

Their story, *Heartbeat for God,* is also remarkable because it shows what God can do through those who totally dedicate themselves to Him and to His service. I pray that, through reading this story of what God has done in and through Elmer and Lee Etta, you, too, will trust God to use you, no matter what your limitations may be.

> Bill Bright
> President and founder
> Campus Crusade for Christ International

Acknowledgements

For many years I dreamed of writing a book to make known all the wonderful things I had seen God do. I claimed this verse: "Publish His glorious acts throughout the earth. Tell everyone about the amazing things He does" (Psalm 96:3, LB).

I am deeply indebted to many people who made this book a reality, from the typists (unknown to me) to Dr. Bill Bright, who first suggested in 1970 that Elmer and I write a book and constantly encouraged us. It was Dr. Bright's example and teachings on the Holy Spirit that literally revolutionized our lives. The stories told in this book are a result of our applying the truths we learned from Dr. Bright.

Many other friends, too numerous to name, prayed for the book and encouraged me along the way. For more than 15 years, my friend Bobbie Taylor and I prayed for the completion of this book. I am especially grateful to her.

Finally, I wish to acknowledge the fine work of the Here's Life Publishers staff of Campus Crusade for Christ, who so faithfully labored to see this book published: Frank Allnutt, Janet Kobobel and especially Maura Card, the writer who spent over a year gathering material and writing the book with me. To her I am particularly indebted, as I found it an impossible task without her assistance.

May God be glorified in whatever is accomplished by publishing this book.

Lee Etta Lappen

This family photo, taken in 1975, shows from left to right, Jon and Bev, standing; with

Chapter 1

Something More Than a Desk Job

It was the afternoon of August 15, 1977. As I waited outside my husband's intensive care hospital room, I kept remembering things I had to do. Tell our senior staff man Elmer's plans for the first week of school. Tell the cleaning woman what to do. Make a grocery list and ask my daughter to shop. Call our friends, Hal and Lana Jones.

"Hal, this is Lee Etta. We can't meet you for dinner tonight. Elmer's in the hospital."

"I'm sorry to hear that," Hal sympathized. "Is his arthritis worse?"

"No. He accidentally fell out of his wheelchair last night and gashed his head," I explained. "There was no concussion, according to the X-rays, but now he's unconscious, and the doctors aren't sure what's wrong. They think he might have had a heart attack."

We talked for a few more minutes. Then Hal said he'd join me at the hospital.

Even though several members of our church staff had waited with me and I had peace that God was taking care of Elmer, I was glad to see Hal. He and his wife had worked on our staff team a few years ago, and I knew that Hal had a special love for Elmer.

We went into Elmer's room, where he lay under an oxygen mask, with a heart monitor attached to his chest. For a couple of moments we quietly watched the rhythmic line of Elmer's heartbeat move across the monitor screen.

'Elmer's Heart Beats for You'

Then we bowed in prayer. "Oh, Lord, we know that Elmer's heart beats for You," Hal prayed. "He's Your servant, totally dedicated to Your will. We believe You want to continue to use him, so we ask that You raise him up and

1

that You would be glorified through it. In Jesus' name we pray. Amen."

I brushed a tear away. Hal's prayer reminded me that one of Elmer's favorite ways to find out about a college student's spiritual condition was to ask, "What's your heartbeat for God?"

And Hal's description of Elmer's walk with God was accurate. Although he'd been crippled with arthritis for 33 of his 53 years, his strong trust in God had led him to have a ministry of evangelism and discipleship with thousands of students. Because Elmer's ministry was so fruitful, I couldn't believe that God wanted it to stop now!

But this wasn't the first accident that had threatened Elmer's ministry. The results of an earlier accident almost caused it not to begin at all . . .

*   *   *

Twenty young men wearing olive green uniforms and helmets charged the giant wooden wall directly ahead as if they were a single force. Carrying backpacks and rifles, they grabbed the knotted ropes hanging from the wall's top and scrambled up the wall. 15 feet high and 50 feet wide, the wall was only the first in a series on an Army combat training obstacle course. It was early March, 1942, and a battalion of Army recruits at Ft. Eustis, Va., was starting its 11th week of a 13-week basic training course.

In the pressure to keep moving and get over the wall quickly, 19-year-old Elmer Lappen slipped near the top of the obstacle. Although he frantically clung to the rope, he plunged backward 12 feet, hitting the ground hard on his hips and lower back.

Pain shot through his body, but Elmer managed to stagger to his feet. Dizzily, he walked around for a couple of moments. Then he saw that most of the other men had cleared the wall and were waiting for the rest to catch up. He *had* to get over that wall and not hold up the exercise!

But Elmer could only move around shakily. Finally he was forced by his numbed body to sit out the rest of the exercise.

Although he tried to ignore it, the pain got worse the next day, so he went to the base hospital. There a doctor X-rayed his back and gave him pills to kill the pain. Little did Elmer know then that this was only the beginning of a lifetime of constant pain.

For more than 35 years, Elmer would have to daily ignore pain to work toward his goal of introducing individuals to Jesus Christ and training them to grow strong in that relationship, just as he'd grown. Yet in spite of spending almost half that time confined to a wheelchair, Elmer would see countless people trust Christ and more than 400 enter full-time Christian work as a result of his ministry.

But Elmer soon did discover that the recurring back pain wasn't as serious as other symptoms that began to develop. Various joints throughout his body, particularly in his feet, became tender, swollen, stiff and painful to move. The base doctors said that Elmer had rheumatoid arthritis, apparently triggered by the accident. But they didn't know how to treat the disease, and Elmer kept working, taking pain pills whenever the pain grew unbearable.

Attacked With a Pie Pan

After basic training, Elmer was assigned to cook's training, and within a year became a mess sergeant in charge of preparing daily meals for 600 men. His first mess sergeant's assignment was at a military prison in Georgia.

One night as dinner was being served, a prisoner demanded more meat. "I'm sorry, soldier," Elmer said, "that's all I'm allowed to give you." The prisoner became furious, grabbed an empty metal pie pan and bounced it off Elmer's head. Elmer was startled, but he wasn't seriously hurt. He watched as two military policemen immediately dragged the prisoner off to the brig, where he received a month of solitary confinement and a diet of bread and water. Elmer was relieved to be transferred to another base before the man was freed.

During the next year and a half, Elmer's arthritis worsened to the point where he found it almost impossible to do any physical work. He applied for a medical discharge and was assigned minor, make-work jobs to keep him busy. Then one day he was told to refill several water buckets that hung high on the barracks walls in case of fire.

As he reached up to rehang a bucket, the pain in his hands grew so sharp that he spilled the whole gallon of water over his head. Frustrated, he threw the bucket on the floor and told his commanding officer that he wasn't able to work any more. His doctor ordered him to stay in bed and gave him pain killers. Two weeks later, Elmer received his medical discharge.

Unsure about what to do with his life, Elmer went home to Philadelphia. Although he temporarily lacked direction, he was confident that God would soon show him what to do.

Elmer's trust in God had begun in 1940, when he was a 17-year-old junior in high school. At that time he began to study the Bible for himself, deciding that the things he'd been taught in church were true and that Jesus Christ really was the Son of God. Soon after this study, Elmer attended a week-long church camp, where he gave his life to Jesus Christ.

Before he became a Christian, Elmer lived for three things — football, basketball and track. He'd worked hard, and as a result, lettered in all three sports. He'd also run in the Penn Relays before thousands of spectators. Now he poured his energy into learning more about his faith.

Because of this earlier commitment, Elmer's pastor and close friend, Dr. Edwin Bustard, challenged him as soon as he got home to consider spending a year at Bible college.

Elmer greatly admired Dr. Bustard, so he took his advice. He entered Philadelphia College of the Bible in 1945 and earned a degree from that school four years later.

Learning to Walk Again

But Elmer's college career was interrupted after the first year and a half. Although he'd grown used to the constant pain of arthritis, his joints were becoming much tighter and inflamed. As a result, he was admitted to a hospital and soon became completely paralyzed.

Despite the fact he couldn't even feed or shave himself, Elmer resisted the temptation to feel sorry for himself. Instead, he asked his nurses to tape Bible verses to a mirror and to place it in such a way that he could study the verses as he lay in bed. Using this method, Elmer memorized more than 300 portions of Scripture during the next year. His belief in God's Word and the visits of his friends gave Elmer strength to trust God through an entire year of hospitalization.

His paralysis didn't last permanently. As movement came back to his joints and Elmer took physical therapy, his therapists helped keep his spirits up with their cheerfulness and hard work. When Elmer was learning how to walk, one therapist urged, "Do you want to walk? Then take just *one* more step before you leave today."

Elmer often joked with his nurses and with his fellow orthopedic ward patients. ("You have to have a sense of humor on an orthopedic ward," Elmer said. "You're all going to be there a while.") "Okay, guys, let's throw this grapefruit around three times," he'd suggest to two men in nearby beds, as he took the fruit out of a basket, "and whoever drops it three times has to peel and eat it." Then Elmer tossed the grapefruit crookedly, saying, "We have to allow for the fact that my arm won't bend."

For excitement, they arranged to get a raw egg and played the same game with it, including the same penalty. Elmer rarely dropped the egg, but when he did, he swallowed it quickly and immediately drank a glass of water to kill its slimey yet bland taste.

But Elmer also experienced times of frustration and discouragement, stemming from the constant pain and from the desire to do more than his disability would allow. "It's always been a battle and something that I periodically struggle with," Elmer said of the frustration shortly before his death. "Even to this day, I have to constantly yield my physical condition to the Lord. It's like a daily dying to self."

But within a few months Elmer conquered his stiff joints and was able to go back to Philadelphia College of the Bible. During the two years following his graduation, Elmer started seminary and was hospitalized three more times.

Then a Veterans Administration counselor advised 28-year-old Elmer to forget about entering the ministry. "Mr. Lappen, you'll never be able to do any type of religious work," the counselor told Elmer, looking at his medical file. "Instead of going back to seminary, you ought to go to business college. You should prepare yourself for a desk job."

As Elmer later thought about that conversation, he realized that heading toward a desk job was the most logical thing to do. Rheumatoid arthritis had already forced him to learn to walk twice as an adult. His doctors had told him that eventually the disease would confine him to a wheelchair. Obviously, with this disability, he couldn't live the active life of a full-time Christian worker for long.

"I know You haven't forsaken me, God," Elmer prayed. "You know I want to serve You full time more than anything else, but now I can't. What do You want me to do now?"

Convinced that God would answer his prayer, Elmer took the V.A. counselor's advice and entered Pierce Business College in Philadelphia. Although he studied hard and made good grades, he hated business college. And his only "vacation" was to be hospitalized for the fourth time.

Experimental Treatments

During his hospital stays, Elmer faced countless experimental treatments and learned to walk again two more times. Although as Elmer's wife I've seen him try many experimental treatments, I still can't imagine what he went through then. These treatments included taking injections of gold compounds, having his legs in casts for six months, receiving hundreds of shots of various serums and being placed in special tanks of hot water.

"I thought the experiments might help me and that, if they helped me, they would bring relief to others," Elmer explained. "I lived in hope that they would find a cure. When one thing failed, I wanted to go on to what was next."

Elmer believes that God used these hospitalizations to help him see life as God sees it. As he ate dinner one night, he realized that both men on either side of him were dying. Elmer estimates that he saw a total of 34 men die during his various hospital stays. These shocking experiences showed him how short life is.

'You're Really Living!'

However, a football game taught Elmer that God's Word is top priority. During one of his hospital stays, a patient gave him two tickets to the Army-Navy football game, one of the biggest games of the year. Elmer, who still loved sports, was excited about the game, all right, but he was even more excited about taking Kathleen, his pretty head nurse. It was his first date in six months. On the day before the game, be bought her a beautiful chrysanthemum corsage, and he was proud of it. On the morning of the game, he was so thrilled that he woke up at 4:30. Later, as Kathleen wheeled him into the stadium, Elmer thought, "Man, Lappen, you're really living!"

Then an official told them, "All the people in wheelchairs must go to the sidelines, and everyone else must sit in the stands. Your friend can't sit with you."

"But sir," Elmer protested, "I haven't had a date in six months!"

"I don't really care," the official answered, repeating the rule.

Reluctantly, Elmer and Kathleen obeyed. At least Elmer still had two consolations: his flower and his game. However, within three minutes of the kickoff, a Navy

player ran right past him for a touchdown. "Remember
that I had been in the Army," Elmer explained to me. "I
wanted to put out my foot to trip that Navy man and bring
him down. Instead, I saw 102,000 fanatics go crazy."

At half-time, Elmer turned around to check on his date
and his flower. "I was sick," he said to me. "Someone had
whalloped Kathleen, and my flower — my beautiful $5
flower — was destroyed. I had figured that each petal cost
3 cents apiece and now there was only about 12 cents
worth of petals left on the corsage. Here I was — with
Army behind in the score 6-0, no girlfriend and with 12
cents of flower left. Then I remembered that there was still
a second half."

But the second half was worse; the final score was
Navy 13, Army 0.

Not wanting to be caught in the crowd, Elmer asked a
man to push his wheelchair into the middle of the field,
where he could wait safely for Kathleen until most of the
people left. There God seemed to speak, "Elmer, aren't
you glad that life is more than just a football game? Remember, 'The grass withers, the flower fades, but the Word
of our God stands forever'" (Isaiah 40:8). "That God's
Word stands forever has burned in my heart from that day
until this," my husband later recalled. "Whenever I stray
from it, the Spirit of God brings it back to my heart."

More Than Business

During the next few months that lesson comforted
Elmer. Still wanting to pursue Christian work instead of
going back to business college, he didn't know what to do
next. One day, Bill and Marian Findieson, some friends
from Florida, visited Elmer. "Why don't you come to St.
Petersburg and spend some time with us when you get out
of the hospital?" they suggested.

Elmer left the hospital in March, 1953, soon after their
visit, and decided to accept their invitation. The trip would
make a good transition in which he could rest and discover
what his next step should be.

The second Sunday after Elmer arrived in St.

Petersburg, he shared his testimony at the Findiesons' church. After the service, businessman Guy Culbreth asked, "Brother Lappen, what do you plan to do with your life?"

"I'm not sure," Elmer answered. "After I leave here, I might take advanced business courses."

"God has more for you than business," Mr. Culbreth insisted.

On the way home that statement continued to ring in Elmer's ears. He felt that God had used Mr. Culbreth's words to tell him, "Elmer, I want all you have. I want to use your life." His desire to serve God would be fulfilled in spite of his physical disability!

While the Findiesons prepared lunch, Elmer sat at the foot of his bed and prayed, "God, if You have more for me than business, let me know. Whatever it is, I'll go with You."

Chapter 2

Trudging Down the Snail Trail

Indeed, God had planned more for Elmer than business. Within three years, together he and I would begin a full-time ministry.

However, during the summer of 1953, Elmer waited for God to show him what to do next. As he waited, he involved himself in every ministry opportunity that presented itself. These included leading a weekly junior church service, preaching in a downtown rescue mission and preaching on a bench at an outdoor church service.

Sensing Elmer's potential in Christian work, two friends urged him to enter Bob Jones University (BJU), their alma mater. He followed their advice, entering the Greenville, S.C., university in fall, 1953.

Thirty-year-old Elmer was older than most of the other BJU students. At first, he was sensitive about the age difference and often felt lonely. Once a fellow student mistook him for a teacher as he walked around campus. However, Elmer made friends with men in his dorm and other students, many of whom nicknamed him "Dad."

Immediately Elmer plunged into various BJU activities. Each dorm roomful of four or five students joined their neighbors across the hall for a nightly prayer meeting, and Elmer was appointed captain of his group. All students belonged to social societies similar to fraternities and sororities; Elmer joined Phi Epsilon Phi, volunteering to coach its intramural basketball team. A sophomore ministerial student (Elmer had been accepted as a sophomore because credits for some of his Bible school courses met freshman course requirements), Elmer preached in a black barber shop each weekend.

On Thanksgiving morning 12 students, including Elmer, shared their testimonies with the 3,000-member BJU student body in a praise service, and I was one of those students in attendance. As I heard Elmer speak of everything God had brought him through, I considered writing a story about him for my radio dramatic writing class. At that time, I had never met Elmer — in fact, I didn't even know his name — and I thought no more about him until that evening.

Walking by Sight

After dinner, my roommate, Joan, who steadily dated another BJU student, talked with me about my love life. A 20-year-old junior, I had casually dated several young men and had just broken up with one of them. Deciding to arrange a date for me, she asked, "Is there anyone on campus you'd like to date?"

"No, I don't think so," I answered. "But I would like to meet the fellow who mentioned learning to walk several times in his testimony this morning." Again, I thought about writing Elmer's story for my class.

The next day Joan told her boyfriend about our conversation. He lived in the same dorm as Elmer did, and that night we went to Elmer's room. "Hey, Elmer," he announced, "there's a girl in Margaret Mack Dorm who wants to date you."

"Who is she?" Elmer asked, surprised.

"She's Lee Etta Durham, my steady's roommate."

"Well, what does she look like?" Elmer asked next. (Elmer used to joke that when potential dates were concerned, he never walked by faith. He preferred to walk by sight, reversing the order of the biblical command.)

They looked up my picture in the previous year's annual. Apparently he thought I didn't look bad, so he wrote me a note asking me out:

Dear Lee Etta,
    Do you, don't you, will you, won't you date me this coming Sunday for food, fun and fellowship?
    Could I meet you Thursday under the clock in the alumni building at 3:30? I will walk you home, and you can tell me then about Sunday.
                    Sincerely,
                    Elmer Lappen

At BJU, men weren't allowed to phone the women's dorms. We communicated via an efficient, society-operated note system in which notes were picked up and delivered to each dorm every evening. Elmer mailed the note as soon as he had finished writing it, and I received it a little later that night.

Making the Date

I was surprised to receive a note from Elmer, since we didn't know each other, but I decided to accept his invitation. That Thursday, despite the rain, I arrived first at the alumni building and waited there for him. Soon I saw Elmer walking toward me. I remember thinking that he was an attractive person — six-feet-one-inch tall, with close-cropped blond hair and with blue eyes that sparkled merrily through his glasses. Although he walked stiffly because of the way the rain affected his arthritic joints, I hardly noticed it.

After a brief greeting, he opened his big black umbrella and we followed several other couples who were inching their way down the Snail Trail, the sidewalk to the women's dorms. This sidewalk was called the Snail Trail because the men walked their dates home so slowly that the constant procession resembled a line of snails.

As we walked to my dorm, Elmer invited me to have dinner with him in the University Tea Room after the Sunday vesper service, and I accepted.

Elmer and I were attracted to each other from that first date. We enjoyed one another's company so much that we soon began to date regularly and talked to each other several times a week.

During our first dates, Elmer and I learned to talk freely with one another. We spent many evenings talking in the dating parlor, a giant living room, replete with chaperones and dozens of comfortable chairs and couches, that covered the entire second floor of the student center. Not content just to discuss surface subjects such as campus activities and our studies, we also shared with each other our backgrounds, our dreams and our goals in life.

Elmer told me that his dad, orphaned at age 13, had dropped out of school to help his older brother support five younger brothers and sisters. By necessity, he became an especially hard worker, a trait that he taught his sons, Elmer and Sam.

Elmer's parents were Christians who were active in their church. Their example and the sudden death of his 15-year-old sister, Anna, one week after she'd trusted Christ caused Elmer to begin to think about God several years before he, too, became a Christian. Later, after he'd trusted Christ, Elmer devoted himself to the church in the same way his parents had. This dedication and his willingness to work hard — both learned from his parents — were among the qualities that initially attracted me to Elmer.

I also admired Elmer's strong desire to tell others about God's love. I'd had the same desire since my freshman year in college, although I'd been a Christian since I was a child.

Searching the Scriptures

I grew up in Dallas, Tex., an only child who attended church every Sunday with my parents. When I was nine years old, I asked my father how old I had to be to join the church. He explained to me that church membership wasn't based on age but instead on having personally established a relationship with Jesus Christ. He quoted me Acts 16:31, ". . . Believe in the Lord Jesus, and you shall be saved, you and your household." I answered that I believed and asked Christ to become my Savior.

However, during the second semester of my freshman year at North Texas State College, the opinions of my social sciences professor caused me to doubt the validity of my Christianity.

One day in class, my professor announced that, since some class members didn't accept some of his teaching due to religious prejudices, we would spend that class session discussing any questions we wanted to ask. In response to our questions, the professor told us that he was an atheist, that there was no eternal life, that Christ couldn't have been born through a virgin birth, that answered prayers were merely accomplishments of our subconscious desires and that the Bible was written by an ancient Egyptian priest.

Because my professor admitted that he'd never read the entire Bible, I determined to read it to decide for myself if the Bible was the Word of God and if I had a firm basis for my faith in Christ. That spring I spent each afternoon reading the New Testament, beginning with the book of Matthew. As I read, I wondered how such a brilliant man as my professor could believe the opposite of what I'd been taught. When I read I Corinthians 1:18,20,21 several weeks later, I found my answer:

> For the word of the cross is to those who are perishing foolishness, but to us who are being saved it is the power of God. . . . Where is the wise man? Where is the scribe? Where is the debater of this age? Has not God made foolish the wisdom of the world? For since in the wisdom of God the world through its wisdom did not come to know God, God was well pleased through the foolishness of the message preached to save those who believe.

From reading that passage, I realized for the first time that there were people who ridiculed Christianity because they didn't know Christ. I'd never thought seriously about this fact because all my friends were Christians. This passage reassured me that I was a Christian since I had trusted Christ. For the first time, my relationship with Jesus Christ became an important part of my life and not just something I took for granted.

New Goals

As a result of my scriptural search, I've never again doubted my salvation or that the Bible is the Word of God. Instead I began to pray often and to find out more of what the Bible teaches. Since I discovered that many people don't know Christ, I gained a deep desire to share my faith with others and to give them an opportunity to know Him. I also began to ask God what my major in college should be and what I should do with my life.

Shortly after I went home for the summer, I told God that He could have my entire life, that I'd do whatever He wanted of me. As I continued to pray, God impressed me that I should transfer to a Christian college and major in Christian education. At first I was reluctant to leave North Texas State College because I was on the school's debate team and had won a national championship. But I wrote to several Christian colleges requesting information, including Bob Jones University. I never received information from most of these schools, but someone at BJU answered my letter immediately.

As I prayed about attending BJU, God gave me peace, in spite of my parents' objection. My parents felt that, at age 18, I was too young to move more than 1,000 miles away from home. As I packed my trunk and made plans to travel by bus to South Carolina, my mother acknowledged that she had dedicated me to God when I was a child and that she had to agree with my decision to go to a Christian college, if that was God's will. Then my father relented and decided to drive me to BJU. For me, this was a confirmation that I'd made the right decision; my parents and I were very close, and I wanted them to approve of what I did.

However, when I arrived at BJU, I was filled with fear because I didn't know anyone. As I walked shakily to the administration building to register, I prayed, "Lord, if You really want me here, cause all my credits from North Texas State to transfer." This would be a miracle, in my opinion; most students lost a few credits when they transferred to a different college. A few moments later I discovered that all my credits had been accepted — even those for a roller skating class I had taken — and I could enter BJU as a sophomore.

My fear also dissolved rapidly as the students I met welcomed me warmly. I liked the students at BJU because they radiated their love for Christ and for other people. In addition to my studies, I participated in many extracurricular activities, which included leading a children's evangelism club, and Theta Delta Omicron, my social society. I was so busy that my sophomore year passed quickly.

Now, during my junior year, I was also dating Elmer. As I learned of Elmer's goals in life, my admiration for him increased. When he told me that he hoped to see at least 100 people enter full-time Christian work as a result of his ministry, I was facinated. I'd never heard anyone share such a goal before.

A Confusing Decision

On one of our early dates, Elmer and I discussed the general subject of marriage and what we expected of a future spouse. He told me that he wanted to marry someone who was strongly committed to Christ. "Lee Ett', the girl I marry will have to be unique," Elmer explained. "Because of my disability, she'll have to help me in many ways, such as typing and driving a car for me."

Suddenly I remembered the words of my eighth grade teacher as she told my class that there were two things everyone should learn to do: to type and to drive a car. My teacher's words had made a big impression on me, and I learned both of these skills in high school. It may sound funny, but I felt that Elmer's mentioning typing and driving was God's first indication that I would marry him.

Elmer and I continued to date throughout the rest of that school year. In June, 1954, we went to Clinton, Tenn., for five days, where I was maid of honor in the wedding of one of my roommates. Elmer and I spent much time together. As a result, I loved him more and Elmer became confused about his feelings for me.

Right after we'd met, Elmer told me that he was writing to a young woman from Florida who had urged him to enter BJU. Unlike many fellows I'd dated, he was honest with me about our relationship at all times and told me where I stood. As our relationship developed, I could see that Elmer enjoyed spending time with me, but that he couldn't commit himself to me because he was confused about whom he should marry. In fact, Elmer says that he occasionally asked his best friend on campus, Ray Hansel, "Which one will it be, Ray, the blonde or the brunette (me)?"

I'd invited Elmer to visit me in Dallas for two weeks, thinking that this visit might help him to make up his mind. As I'd prayed about our relationship during the past several months, I kept receiving direction from the Lord that Elmer and I would marry. Because of this consistent direction, I was puzzled that Elmer didn't know he would marry me, as well as discouraged that our relationship wasn't progressing as quickly as I'd hoped it would.

Special News

However, Elmer's visit didn't help him make a choice, although we both enjoyed our time together. Our relationship seemed to have come to a halt, and I became more frustrated.

Several weeks later, on September 12, shortly after the fall semester began, Elmer and I went to the dating parlor to discuss the relationship. "There's no point in our dating when you can't make up your mind," I told him. As a result, we decided to stop dating, except to attend Elmer's Phi Epsilon Phi outing on October 23, until Elmer could choose the girl he loved more. This separation was hard for me because I loved Elmer, and I felt that God was leading us together. Yet I didn't see any other alternative.

Elmer and I both dated different people. Occasionally we saw each other on our way to classes or at the library, where I worked. One day, when I was sick and confined to the infirmary, Elmer realized, when he didn't see me that day, that he had been watching for me. He asked two friends if they knew where I was and found out that I was sick. Then he wrote me a get well note, the first note in almost a month. In it, he reminded me of our date on October 23 and asked for an all-day date on the day after that. I wrote back, confirming both dates.

Four nights later, on October 7, Elmer thought about me so much that he couldn't sleep. As he told me later, he thought of how we'd met, the fun we'd had together and

how we'd parted. Suddenly he realized that he loved me —
and he couldn't wait to tell me of his decision.

Since students were required to turn out their lights by
11 p.m., and it was now long past that time, Elmer got out
of bed, fumbled in the dark for a pen and stationery and
sneaked into the restroom, the only place in the dorm that
was still lighted. He glanced at his watch and noticed that
it was 3 a.m. Then he wrote me this note:

> Dear Lee Etta,
> This letter is brief and to the point. I want to say I love
> you with *all* my heart. Needless to say, I want to see you
> and talk with you as soon as possible. Haven't been able
> to sleep for a couple of nights very well. Will try to explain
> things when we see each other. I never have been com-
> pletely happy since September 12th, when we said good-
> bye to each other.
> God knows my heart. I hope you will forgive me.
> Remember, I love you with my whole heart.
> > Love,
> > Elmer

After breakfast that morning, he handed me the note
and asked if he could walk me to my dorm. I read it as we
sauntered down the Snail Trail. Then he told me that he
realized he loved me and that he wanted to marry me. He
asked me to marry him the following June, suggesting
that we become officially engaged at Christmas.

A $5 Wedding Veil

Although I knew I'd say "yes," I asked Elmer to let me
think about it for a few days and then I'd give him an
answer. Three days later, after I'd prayed and spoken to
the campus minister, I agreed to marry Elmer.

Our parents reacted favorably to the news that we
were engaged. However, my parents wanted me to consider seriously what it would be like to live with Elmer's
handicap. I assured them that I realized it would be difficult at times, but that God had led us together and that
He would take care of any problems. Besides, I loved
Elmer and believed that love would conquer anything.

At Christmas, Elmer visited me in Dallas and brought my engagement ring. Before he arrived, just for fun, my mother and I window shopped for a wedding dress. In the window of a ritzy department store I found the ideal wedding dress — and it was marked down to half price. I tried on the dress, and it fit perfectly. Then I found a wedding veil that matched the ivory-colored dress, and it was marked down from $22.95 to $5. I paid a $5 deposit to hold the dress and veil, and paid for them on layaway. Finding the dress and veil confirmed to my mother that God was in my engagement to Elmer. I couldn't afford to spend a large amount, and it was a miracle that I was able to buy on sale the dress and veil that I would have chosen if I'd had unlimited money to spend.

On June 1, 1955, I walked down two aisles. In the morning I graduated *cum laude* from BJU, receiving a B.A. in humanities, and in the afternoon I married Elmer. Dr. Bob Jones, Sr. performed our wedding ceremony, and Elmer's beloved pastor, Dr. Bustard, came all the way from Philadelphia to pray in our wedding.

That fall I taught all the subjects in an eighth grade class as Elmer began his senior year at Bob Jones University.

Then, during the spring of 1956, Elmer and I began to pray about what we should do after Elmer graduated in June. Shortly before graduation, some deacons from a small North Carolina church interviewed Elmer. These men were certain that Elmer was the perfect pastor for their church and another small church (in some rural areas, a pastor would often shepherd two tiny churches). His dedication, experience and training impressed them. However, Elmer and I were unsure about whether to accept this pastorate and continued to seek God's will for our ministry.

A Four-minute Interview

Soon after Elmer had talked with these deacons, he received a call slip from the dean, notifying him that if he was interested in talking with Bill Bright, the founder and president of Campus Crusade for Christ, to come to the dean's office that afternoon. At that time, Elmer wasn't interested in the interview and tore up the message. The next day he received another call slip asking him to speak to Mr. Bright. Since the dean had sent him two messages about this opportunity, Elmer decided to follow it up.

He joined 20 other young men whom Mr. Bright told briefly about the five-year-old ministry of Campus Crusade, an organization that sought to disciple and evangelize college students. After this presentation, Mr. Bright asked to speak individually with Elmer and two others whom the dean had recommended. These talks would also be short, Mr. Bright explained, because he had to leave immediately to follow up a football coach and eight players at the University of South Carolina. They had received Christ at a recent evangelistic meeting he had conducted with their team. This explanation grabbed Elmer's attention because he still loved athletics, and in those days, one didn't hear of many individual athletes becoming Christians, much less a coach and eight players receiving Christ at the same time. "Is this something that I could do, too?" Elmer wondered.

"Are you aware that I have rheumatoid arthritis?" Elmer asked Mr. Bright.

"Yes, the dean has told me about you."

"Mr. Bright, you couldn't place me in Arizona, where the weather would be good for my health, could you?"

"I couldn't," Bill Bright answered, "but maybe the Lord could. Let's pray about it."

After they prayed together, Mr. Bright gave Elmer an application and some literature about Campus Crusade and left. Elmer looked at his watch; the interview had lasted only four minutes.

That evening Elmer showed me the literature and told me all he knew about Campus Crusade. He was attracted to the possibility of working with athletes through the student ministry. However, the organization was still young and we'd be required to raise part of our small salary. For us, this opportunity represented the adventure of facing the unknown, because it was unlike anything we'd ever done before. In addition, we were required to attend the ministry's Staff Training Institute in Los Angeles, on August 1. This looked impossible because we were expecting the birth of our first child on July 7.

Two Threatening Obstacles

Accepting the pastor's position in the two churches represented security. We'd receive a guaranteed salary and would work out of a church building. Yet we knew that the humid North Carolina climate was bad for Elmer's arthritis.

We faced a difficult decision. Both opportunities would equally honor the Lord and allow us to serve Him full time. Both had advantages and disadvantages, and we felt no strong attraction to either. During the next few weeks we prayed often: Which opportunity should we take?

If one can't determine God's will in any other way, we discovered, God often leads through circumstances. Two weeks before Elmer's final examinations, the weather turned rainy; then his arthritis made him completely immobile. I had to feed and shave him, and he spent a few days in the BJU infirmary. It became obvious to us that Elmer wouldn't be able to minister effectively in the humid, rainy North Carolina climate.

After Elmer could move and returned to classes a few days later, we applied to join Campus Crusade for Christ staff. We were notified by the end of May that we'd been accepted on the ministry's staff and that we were assigned to Arizona State College in Tempe, Ariz.

However, two obstacles threatened our new calling. We'd have to sell our trailer home at a time when no one was buying such trailers. Also, the date by which we'd have to leave for our training would be too soon after the birth of our baby. I wouldn't be strong enough by then to pack for our move to Arizona, take care of my husband and new baby, and drive almost 3,000 miles to Los Angeles for Staff Training.

Once again, Elmer and I prayed, asking God to solve our problems. Within a few days, these obstacles were removed — but their solutions came in ways that we didn't expect.

Chapter 3

Go Ye Therefore to Arizona

As Elmer, his parents and I were eating dinner in a restaurant, I announced, "Something happened and I'd better go to the hospital."

"Do you mean the baby's coming?" Elmer asked, looking nervous. His parents had come for his graduation from BJU, and tonight we were celebrating our first wedding anniversary. The baby couldn't come now!

But I answered that it was.

"Then why are you eating your pie so calmly? We'd better get out of here quick!"

"I can't drive right now," I reminded him. "You'll have to find someone to take me to the hospital." I was the only one of the four of us who drove.

Elmer looked frantically around the restaurant and saw a young couple who lived in our trailer court. He quickly explained our problem, and they immediately drove us to the hospital.

It was a false alarm, and my doctor sent me back home. "Stay in bed for a few days until labor starts," he told me. What a disappointment — our anniversary party had been cut short and the baby hadn't come after all!

I took the doctor's advice, and nearly a week later, on June 7, I went to the hospital again. This time it wasn't a wasted trip. Elmer and I had a seven-pound son, Jonathan Edwin Lappen. How thrilled we were!

"Jonathan" means "gift of God," and our new baby was truly a gift of God in several ways. We were excited just to have our first child — a beautiful, healthy son. And, even though Jon had been born a whole month early, he was a normal-sized baby. Plus, because Jon *had* been born early, he'd be old enough to travel six weeks later, when we had to leave for California.

Jon's being born early would also give me more time to

regain my strength. Maybe I'd be strong enough to pack for our move and drive across country after all.

Confirming the Call

But we still needed to sell our trailer, and our chance of selling it was slim. In Greenville, only students lived in trailers, and since it was summer, there were no new students who needed to buy a mobile home. Too, our trailer was old, and I knew of at least a dozen just like it that were also for sale. Still I posted a 3 X 5" card in our trailer court's laundry room announcing that our trailer was for sale. That night my mother and I prayed that we could sell it. (Mom had come to help me with the new baby.)

After we'd finished praying, someone knocked at the door. A young couple from Ohio who were coming to college that fall had seen my little sign and wanted to look at our trailer. I gladly showed them around. "We *might* come back," the couple said as they left to look at another trailer.

To my amazement, the young couple came back 15 minutes later. "We liked your trailer better than any others we've looked at," they said. "We'll take it." They even paid us the exact amount we'd paid a year before!

Elmer and I were excited about how God had confirmed our call to Campus Crusade staff. When Elmer got out of the hospital, where he'd been receiving arthritis treatments, we waited eagerly to see how God would handle our problem with moving. We needed to pack all our belongings for a permanent move, and neither Elmer nor I could lift anything heavy. But our neighbors pitched in to help us pack, loading everything into the U-Haul we'd rented. Now we were ready to set out for our new ministry.

Traveling across the country wasn't easy for me. I had to do all the driving, and I'd never pulled a trailer before. We had to stop often — making a long, hot trip even longer — to feed Jon or to change his diapers. Yet we enjoyed the trip, even though it was tiring for us. I've always loved to drive, and I thrive on challenges. We saw our trip, new ministry and the new life-style it brought as adventures.

Unexpected treats along the way helped us survive the heat. One day we stopped, parched, hungry and dusty, at a roadside watermelon stand somewhere in west Texas. There we bought the sweetest, juiciest, *best*, yellow-meat watermelon we've ever eaten. In fact, years later, we sometimes still talked about how good that melon was.

Our excitement even carried us through our short, hectic stop in Tempe. There we quickly found a tiny apartment close to the Arizona State College campus. A college friend helped us unload our things, and we drove on to Los Angeles and Staff Training.

Meeting 'Movie Stars'

On the first night of Staff Training, 55 of us, half volunteers and half full-time staff, gathered in a church near the UCLA campus where we would have all our meetings for the next three weeks. We were all living in a sorority house Campus Crusade had rented.

I hadn't met Bill Bright when Elmer did, and I was awed when I saw Bill in his white dinner jacket and his wife, Vonette, in her semiformal red dress. "They look like movie stars," I thought. In spite of their glamorous looks, I found the Brights very warm and personable. They had a contagious dedication and vision for helping to tell the entire world about Jesus Christ. They also had an evident love for people and were always available to us. I soon saw that they didn't always dress like movie stars. Normally they dressed more casually — Bill in sport shirts and slacks, and Vonette in dresses.

Our next three weeks of training kept us very busy. Each staff member was assigned to teach the rest from a book of Bible doctrine, and I taught on stewardship. I was able to participate in all the sessions since I could leave Jon in a nursery that the ministry had provided. We spent at least eight hours a day in meetings, which included the lessons on doctrine, sessions on methods of evangelism and discipleship, and inspirational speakers. The conference emphasized being empowered by the Holy Spirit, and Bill Bright gave a series of talks on this principle.

I think the Lord allowed Jon to be born early just so I could attend Staff Training and understand what it means to be controlled by the Holy Spirit. I hadn't had any teaching about the Holy Spirit before. As I listened to Bill's messages, I learned who the Holy Spirit is, why He came and how to be filled with the Spirit. I began to realize that the Holy Spirit is God, the Third Person of the Trinity, and the very moment we trust Christ as our Savior, He comes to live in us. I saw that He leads us as we allow Him to, and our yielding to His direction is what it means to be filled with the Holy Spirit.

Confess and Trust

In Ephesians 5:18, Bill pointed out to us, we are commanded to be filled with the Spirit. The tense of the Greek word for "filled" in this verse means that we are to be continually filled, that we can be filled with the Spirit many times, not just once.

But first I had to confess any known sin to God before He would fill me with His power. In I John 1:9, we're commanded to confess our sins and promised forgiveness when we do: "If we confess our sins, He is faithful and righteous to forgive us our sins and to cleanse us from all unrighteousness."

"Confess" means to say the same thing about our sins that God says. I saw for the first time that if I was willing to admit that my sin was sin, instead of calling it a fault or human weakness, then I was on my way to victory.

After I confessed my sin, the next step was to trust the Holy Spirit to control and empower me. By faith, I had to believe that God had filled me with His Spirit and that I now had the power to witness and to live for Him.

Since those days in Staff Training, I've recognized that if I hadn't come to understand the Spirit-filled life when I did, Elmer and I probably would have left Campus Crusade staff in defeat after our first year. After all, I was scared to witness to college "intellectuals"; we had problems getting our ministry officially recognized on campus; and our director went to another part of the state after our first couple of months in Arizona, leaving us to direct the ministry at Arizona State College — even though we felt like mere rookies.

But we had been carefully prepared for a ministry during Staff Training, with training in witnessing that taught us how to use a religious survey to open a conversation about Christ. We also memorized "God's Plan for Your Life," a typed, 10-page gospel message from which the Four Spiritual Laws booklet would be condensed nearly 10 years later. (See Appendix A.)

'Who's Dick?'

At first, several of the new staff, including Elmer and me, balked at memorizing God's Plan. Since we'd had Bible college training we wanted to use our own knowledge and logic instead. But experienced staff assured us that the talk was very effective, and we memorized it.

A few days later, we went out two by two into the community and on the UCLA campus to try the survey and God's Plan. Most of the new staff hadn't finished memorizing the message, and we didn't feel prepared to witness. Yet when we came together afterward to share our experiences, we found that several people had trusted Christ in spite of our fears.

One new staff man had talked with a UCLA student sitting on a lawn. After he had asked the questions in the survey, he asked, "Has it ever occurred to you, Dick, that God loves you and has a wonderful plan for your life?" Then he presented the rest of God's Plan. At the end, the staff man asked the student if he would like to receive Christ.

"Yes I would," the student answered. "But I have a question: Who is this fellow 'Dick' you keep talking about?"

We all roared with laughter. Whenever "Dick" was mentioned in God's Plan, we were supposed to substitute the name of the person we were talking with, but the nervous new staff member didn't manage to make that transition.

On the last night of the conference we all packed into
Bill and Vonette's home for a final dedication program. We
lit candles and placed them on a world map. This sym-
bolized our desire for God to use us to help fulfill the Great
Commission of our Lord to "go into all the world and
preach the gospel to all creation" (Mark 16:5). Elmer and I
also chose to claim John 15:16 for our ministry: "You did
not choose Me, but I chose you, and appointed you, that
you should go and bear fruit, and that your fruit should
remain; that whatever you ask of the Father in My name,
He may give to you."

Settling In

Elmer and I went back to Tempe in late August, in-
spired by Staff Training and excited about starting our
ministry with college students. We weren't very impressed
with our new home state at first because the Arizona
desert was so hot, dusty and barren. The only green trees
and lawns we saw were right in the heart of town where
there was irrigation. Many people had desert lawns —
sand and rocks with arrangements of various types of
cacti. We hadn't paid much attention to these things when
we'd stopped here before; our minds were on finding a
place to live and getting to Staff Training.

When our friend Dick Williams came over to help us
unpack, Elmer asked him, "Is it always this hot here?" The
temperature was a broiling 108 degrees, and we felt mis-
erable. "You'll get used to it," he assured us.

Later, we'd see that the hot climate was actually to our
advantage. It was easier to start conversations about
Christ with students who were outside, and almost all
year we could find many students involved in outdoor
activities, or casually sitting on benches and lawns between classes.

Elmer, Jon and I soon made ourselves at home in our
tiny apartment and got to know the other two staff members we'd work with at Arizona State College. They were
Austin Mathis (Matty), our director, and Irene Van
Bochove.

Although Arizona State College wasn't the most strategic place for a ministry in terms of size — its enrollment then was only 6,800 — a local carpenter, Cecil Redden, had asked Campus Crusade to start a ministry there. Mr. Redden's son, Ralph, had been convinced that Arizona State needed a Campus Crusade group because of the ministry's strong emphasis on discipleship and evangelism. After Ralph was killed in a plane crash, Mr. Redden remembered Ralph's conviction and offered his son's insurance money to pay the first staff member's salary for a year. Matty was assigned to start the ministry at Arizona State in 1955, and he was the only staff member there until Irene, Elmer and I joined him a year later. Since few had heard of Campus Crusade, Matty spent his first year telling students and laymen about it and organizing an advisory board of local businessmen. Now the four of us would actually start working with students.

Arizona State was different from any campus I'd ever been on. It was a melting pot of white, black, Chicano and Indian students — and there was no conflict between the races. Cowboy togs and squaw dresses were popular on campus, especially whenever there was a rodeo in nearby Phoenix. Then if anyone on campus was caught not wearing western clothes, students would lasso him and put him into a corral for punishment until they felt like letting him go. I didn't have any western clothes, and I was afraid I'd be captured, but I never was.

'She's a Communist'

At first I was afraid to witness on the college campus, although Elmer was ready to plunge right in. Most of the witnessing I'd done before had been to children. I was scared that everyone I'd meet on campus would be an intellectual who would give me a hard time.

Also, as a new mother, I felt Elmer's calling was to go to campus and mine was to stay home with the baby. I didn't want to leave Jon with the babysitters, but Elmer insisted that I make some appointments with girls to talk about Christ, and I did. After I saw that God would use me as I talked with students and as I claimed His wisdom, I gradually overcame my fear of witnessing.

As it turned out, I didn't even have to leave Jon with ordinary babysitters. On the afternoons I went to campus, Elmer stayed with him, using the time Jon slept to rest, plan for the ministry or write letters. Whenever Elmer couldn't stay with Jon, my neighbor kept an eye on him.

Before I'd resolved my struggle, two of my first campus experiences made it harder. That fall I spent two afternoons a week with students. At that time, Campus Crusade wasn't an officially recognized religious group on campus, and the students didn't know who we were and what we were doing. A few weeks after classes had started, I met a student named Donna Cox at a church dinner for college students. I phoned her a few days later to make an appointment to go through a survey and to tell her about Jesus Christ. This is what I usually did whenever I first met students.

At that time, I didn't know that someone had tacked up this sign on the bulletin board in Donna's dorm: "If a lady calls you and asks to have a Coke and take a religious survey with you, DON'T GO! She's a communist."

Donna had seen the sign and was a little scared to talk to me. But when I asked for an appointment, she agreed to meet me.

The day of our appointment, Donna told her roommates what she was going to do, and when I came to pick up Donna, they took down my car's license number in case anything happened to her.

After we finished our Cokes, we sat in my car, and I shared God's Plan with her. Then Donna accepted Christ — my first Arizona State convert! Later she told me about the sign and that she'd been scared I was a communist.

Kicked Out of the Dorm

A few weeks later, Donna and I were having a follow-up Bible study in her dorm lounge when a housemother came over and asked, "Who are you and what are you doing?"

"I'm Lee Etta Lappen," I said, surprised. "We're having a Bible study."

"What group are you with?"

"Campus Crusade for Christ."

"I've never heard of it," the housemother snapped. "Since you don't represent a recognized religious group, you'll have to leave and have your Bible study somewhere else."

I went home in tears. However, Donna and I continued to meet somewhere else, and she grew strong in her relationship with Jesus Christ. Later, when churches invited Campus Crusade staff and students to speak in their services, Donna often went with us.

Since meeting students on campus was vital to our ministries, Matty and Elmer immediately applied for Campus Crusade to become an official campus religious group. At first a couple of organizations in the campus religious association opposed us and this held up our applications for several weeks. The association had to vote unanimously to officially accept us.

'Let Me Stay Here'

While we waited for official status, we continued to meet students outside campus buildings and off campus. Matty, Irene and I all saw students receive Christ with us and were having Bible studies with some of them, but Elmer hadn't yet experienced this. He was frustrated because he wanted badly to help students to know Jesus Christ personally, and he'd spent as much time witnessing as Matty and Irene had.

One Monday morning during our weekly staff meeting, we decided to go up to Prescott, in northern Arizona, to look at a potential campsite for a retreat we were planning. The trip would take several hours, so we wouldn't have a chance to go to Arizona State that day.

On the day of the trip, Elmer begged off. "Why don't the three of you go and make the decision without me?" he suggested. "Let me stay here and witness." I don't think he could bear to go through another day without seeing someone trust Christ. He didn't have any assurance that this would happen, but he was certainly willing to share his faith that day and find out.

So Matty, Irene and I left for Prescott. Elmer prayed and headed off to campus, wondering whom he'd have an opportunity to talk to that day.

Chapter 4

On Our Own

As Elmer walked down College Avenue, the main road through Arizona State College, he spotted a student sitting alone on a white stone bench. Elmer immediately recognized him as one of the campus baseball team's best hitters, and went over to him.

"You're Joe Thomas, aren't you?" Elmer asked. "My name is Elmer Lappen, and I work with Campus Crusade for Christ. I really admire your playing ability. How's practice going?"

Elmer and Joe talked for a few minutes about the Sun Devils' prospects for the coming season. Then Elmer said, "Joe, I'm taking a collegiate religious survey, and I'd like to get your opinions, if you have a few minutes."

"Sure," Joe answered. "Go ahead."

Elmer went through the survey, asking Joe if he was a member of a religious group, how often he presently attended services, which religious founder he knew the most about, who Jesus Christ was according to his understanding and how he'd gained that understanding. Then Elmer asked, "Joe, do you feel the need for a more personal religious faith?"

"Yeah," Joe answered thoughtfully. "I guess everybody does at some time."

"That's interesting, because many of the students I talk to feel the same way," Elmer continued. "Could I share with you how you *can* have a more personal religious faith? It makes a lot of sense to most students."

"I'd like that."

Elmer began to talk through God's Plan, which we had memorized at Staff Training, but the presentation took longer than usual. They were sitting in the busiest part of campus and several of Joe's passing friends came up and interrupted. Elmer realized too late that they should have gone to a more private place to talk.

Yet he managed to finish telling Joe about Jesus Christ. And when Elmer asked him if he wanted to invite Christ to come into his life, the baseball player indicated that he would and prayed with Elmer.

Two Types of Christians

After that talk, Elmer's ministry seemed to pick up, and he saw several other students become Christians in the following months. He also began to find Christian students whom he could encourage to grow in their faith. Some were eager to walk closely with Christ, Elmer discovered, and others weren't quite ready to make that commitment.

The first committed student Elmer met was Jim Rosscup, a sports writer for Arizona State's campus newspaper. They met one day in front of a dorm, and when Elmer suggested that they get together for Bible study, Jim welcomed the opportunity. Jim's excitement about his faith constantly encouraged Elmer during our rough first year on staff. Not only was Jim willing to go with Elmer to witness to other students — and many weren't willing to do that — but he also shared the good news on his own.

Shortly after Elmer met Jim, our ministry was officially recognized and Jim became its first student chairman. To Elmer's joy, Jim's participation in Christian activities continued after he graduated, and he's now a professor at Talbot Seminary in California.

On the other hand, Milt Pope, a freshman engineering student, didn't exactly start off blazing in his relationship with Christ. Although he was a Christian, he didn't want others to know it, and he refused to be seen with Elmer on campus because Elmer was a Christian worker. However, Milt *was* willing to have coffee and a few moments of Bible study with Elmer at restaurants far from campus.

Elmer and I always gave new Christians materials containing basic principles of the Christian life and tried to get together with them again for follow-up. In follow-up appointments we discussed assurance of salvation, how to grow in Christ and how to be filled with the Holy Spirit.

Sometimes we assigned new Christians a Bible verse to memorize before the next appointment. Naturally, this is what Elmer tried to do with Milt.

Shooting Spiritual BB's

But Elmer soon discovered that students who hadn't done their assignments would conveniently not show up for follow-up sessions, and Milt was one of these students. To motivate him to come anyway, Elmer told him, "Milt, I'd really like you to memorize this verse before we get together again. But if for some reason you can't, we'll work on it together and talk about it when we meet." Then Milt began to meet Elmer regularly.

Elmer called this Scripture memorization "shooting spiritual BB's into students." I was satisfied if I could shoot one spiritual BB a week into kids like Milt. Elmer recalled, "That way I could help a guy who wouldn't do his work to start growing anyway."

Once when Elmer and Milt were talking in a campus lounge after a Bible study session, a man came in to fill up a Coke machine. When the man rattled his Coke bottles, Milt jumped because he was so jittery about being seen with a Christian worker on campus. (Elmer had his Bible with him.)

Yet eventually Elmer's patience paid off, and Milt Pope's commitment to Christ grew. "At first I was lucky that Milt would meet me at all," Elmer said. "Then slowly but surely, he realized that we loved him, and he came around. Within the next year he developed into a real leader, both in Christian activities and on the campus. He became our student chairman after Rosscup and later got Christians into the student government." As a graduate student, Milt later helped launch a ministry at the University of Arizona in Tucson. After earning a Ph.D. at Stanford, he became an actively witnessing layman.

During our first few years on staff, most of the Christian students we met were uncommitted, as Milt had been at first. Many of the students we worked with were friends who came to our group meetings for fellowship but never involved themselves further. Bob Adams was like this at first, but he turned out to be an exception.

Bob's uncle had asked us to look him up, and Elmer shared Christ with him. Bob didn't want to become a Christian then, but he began to come to our house several times a week. He liked spending time with us, and often he brought along friends "who need to hear what you tell them," even though he didn't yet believe our message himself. Several of Bob's friends became Christians with Elmer, but five months passed before Bob did so himself.

After Bob finally trusted Christ, he grew steadily in his faith. Now, more than 20 years later, he still actively serves Christ as a layman in his local church and has served as president of his denomination's state convention.

We Become Directors

Near the end of our first semester at Arizona State, Matty told us that he and Irene were moving to Tucson to start a ministry at the University of Arizona. As Campus Crusade state director for Arizona, he had the freedom to manage that ministry however he thought best — even if it meant leaving his assigned campus for another. Since we'd helped to start the ministry at Arizona State and Elmer and I would be there to keep it going, Matty felt it was important to start another ministry at the University of Arizona.

"Oh no!" Elmer and I immediately thought. We weren't ready to run a ministry yet! Our Staff Training had taught us how to open a conversation about Jesus Christ, how to share the gospel and how to do basic follow-up with new Christians. But there were so many other practical lessons we needed to learn about conducting evangelistic meetings, leading Bible studies, discipling individuals and planning workable strategies to reach our campus for Christ. We didn't think we'd been at Arizona State long enough to know what things would and wouldn't work there. Elmer and I were scared to be on our own, but we both wanted to trust God to show us how to direct the ministry.

It's a good thing I'd resolved my struggle about witnessing because now I *had* to minister to college girls. "Honey, if you don't go to campus, we won't have any girls' work," Elmer reminded me on days when I wanted to stay home. "It wouldn't be right for me to be working with those girls."

I knew he was right, and to make this possible, we made our shared babysitting a daily practice: Elmer worked with students during the mornings and came back in the afternoons to plan, rest and stay with Jon while I went to campus in the afternoons. Often when I got back home, I'd find Elmer doing little things to help with dinner, such as peeling potatoes.

Trial and Error

Learning to direct the ministry was a process of trial and error. One of the first things we learned was how to set priorities and stick to them. As Campus Crusade staff, we were required to help raise finances for our personal ministries and that of our particular campus, although Bill Bright handled most of the fund raising at that time. To meet people and acquaint them with our ministry, we accepted every group speaking opportunity anywhere in Arizona that we could get.

God used us to encourage various churches and other Christian groups, and we gained some financial and prayer support. But in the process we got so tired that we couldn't effectively carry out the campus ministry that God had called us to. We soon realized that the campus was our priority, so we began to limit the number of outside speaking engagements we accepted. Except for money for special events — such as an evangelistic student leadership banquet — we limited our support development to summertime, when there were no campus activities.

Elmer was intrigued with the idea of trying team meetings, in which an emcee, one or two people sharing

testimonies and a main speaker conducted an evangelistic
meeting with a specialized group. Elmer's target groups
were the campus football team and fraternities. But he
didn't know how to get started.

When we went to a three-day staff retreat in Oklahoma during the Christmas holidays, Elmer pumped a
senior staff member for all his insights on doing team
meetings. Although our tiny staff handbook included in-
struction, Elmer wanted to learn firsthand from someone
who had been successful, and this staff member had seen
many trust in Christ through team meetings.

After we got home from the retreat, Elmer took a
student with him to visit fraternity presidents. In their
enthusiasm, they lined up eight team meetings to be held
in the next few weeks. Then it struck Elmer that now he'd
have to speak at all those meetings. Although he knew
God's Plan well and used it daily in witnessing to individuals, he was nervous about sharing it with entire
fraternities. After all, fraternity men were supposed to
learn to be leaders.

Ups and Downs

During the few days before the first team meeting,
Elmer constantly practiced God's Plan in front of a mirror.
He was so anxious about it that when I called him for
dinner one night he said, "Not now, hon. I've got to know
this thing perfectly."

On the night of the first meeting, Elmer and the two
men who were giving their testimonies met at our apartment for prayer. Then they nervously set out for the
fraternity. As they were about to go in, they heard someone say, "Quick, hide the bottles! Here they come!" Yet the
meeting itself went well, and a couple of men trusted
Christ. The team came back to our apartment both relieved and rejoicing.

Not all of the team meetings ran so smoothly. Elmer
always had a hard time getting up out of chairs, and he
usually braced himself by his arm and pushed himself up
with one leg. As Milt Pope introduced Elmer as the
speaker at one meeting, Elmer tried to get up, slipped on

the freshly-waxed floor and fell flat. But he wasn't hurt, and he quipped as he got up, "Well, men, that's the way life is. It has its ups, and it has its downs." Then he launched into God's Plan, and several men became Christians that night.

Praise God for Problems

Another thing we learned during our first years on Campus Crusade staff was how to praise God for problems. Elmer would phone Bill Bright long distance whenever we ran into ministry problems that we didn't know how to handle. We phoned him when I was kicked out of the dorm and several times during the weeks when we didn't know if our ministry would be officially recognized on campus or not.

We also called Bill when a dean threatened to cancel our promotional banquet to introduce Campus Crusade to local laymen. It was scheduled to be held in the student union building the week before finals — a week when no student activities were allowed. We hadn't thought this rule applied to our banquet because the only students involved were a few who were on the program. So we were horrified when the dean canceled it only a week in advance.

As Elmer told Bill about this problem, Bill listened carefully and then enthusiastically said the same thing he always said, "Praise the Lord!" He *constantly* emphasized that we were to praise God no matter what happened. Bill told us that God would work out all our problems if we'd give them to Him in prayer and praise Him for them. Then he prayed with us.

Finally Elmer and I got the message. The next time we faced an obstacle, Elmer suggested, "Why don't we just praise the Lord ourselves and save the phone bill?" And we did.

Our banquet wasn't canceled after all. Elmer took Milt with him to visit the dean. After Milt shared what our ministry had meant to him and convinced her that only a few students would participate, she decided to let us have our banquet as planned.

In addition to praising God for our problems, we learned to entrust problems to God and to obey Him in everything. God used a new car to teach us these things. On Wednesdays, Elmer and I went to Phoenix College (PC), a local junior college, to lead a weekly Christian club meeting and to take some of the club members witnessing. One day was particularly discouraging because we didn't see anybody trust Christ with us, and one student we'd shared with gave us a hard time. As Elmer and I left PC, we decided to look at new Pontiacs at a friend's dealership just for fun.

Stranded on New Year's Eve

Those new cars looked tempting. We didn't need a new car then because ours was only a year old, in good condition and had been driven only 12,000 miles. But on the spur of the moment, to console ourselves for our frustrating day at PC, we traded in our car for a brand new Pontiac station wagon.

We bought the car right before our Christmas staff retreat in Oklahoma, and Elmer, Jon, Matty, Irene and I went to the retreat in the new car. We were driving home late on New Year's Eve when our brand new car broke down in the middle of nowhere. We couldn't imagine what was wrong.

"I hope we can hitchhike to town," Matty said. The nearest town was Safford, Arizona, 20 miles away.

"What if we're stuck here for hours," I complained. "No one'll *ever* pick up hitchhikers on New Year's Eve! The baby will get too cold in the car."

"Well, at least we won't starve," Irene chirped. "The Lord knew what was going to happen when we bought those groceries in Lordsburg.

The rest of us were almost annoyed with Irene. She was *always* praising the Lord in everything. Obviously she didn't understand how serious our predicament was!

Matty got out to find help, and within a few minutes he'd flagged down a car. The driver, a schoolteacher from Safford, and Matty tinkered with the stalled car. They couldn't figure out the problem, so the teacher took Matty, Jon and me to Safford with him. Matty would bring back help, and I was going to a college friend's home to keep Jon warm.

My friend, Elaine Eggleston, received us graciously, even though she wasn't expecting us, and her brother went back with Matty to help fix our car. Although Elaine's brother had some experience with car repairs, he couldn't get the car started either. So they left the car there overnight, and we all spent the night with the Egglestons.

'Some Trust in Chariots'

While I was getting ready for bed, Psalm 20:7 popped into my mind: "Some boast (or trust) in chariots, and some in horses; but we will boast in the name of the Lord our God." Had Elmer and I been "trusting in chariots"?

We realized then that buying our new car was sin because we'd bought it for all the wrong reasons. We hadn't trusted God with our frustrating day, we didn't seek God's will about the car's purchase, and we didn't even need it. Also, we were putting an unnecessary strain on our finances. We'd owned our previous car, and payments for the new one were $100 a month — about one-third of our monthly salary!

Now we understood that God wanted us to walk in His Spirit *all* the time, to trust Him with everything in our personal lives, as well as everything in our ministry. That night Elmer and I prayed together, confessing our sin, asking God to direct us and to take care of our car problems.

The next day Elaine's brother took us back to our car. The moment he checked it again, he found a loose bolt, tightened it and the car started right up. Soon we were on our way home.

I don't think the new station wagon was a lemon. Rather, I believe God allowed that bolt to come loose just to show Elmer and me that we had to trust and obey Him in everything.

A Solid Start

I can't say that we saw a dramatic change in our ministry after that lesson. But we were growing in Christ ourselves, and we saw more students become Christians and start to grow. That first year at Arizona State, about 50 students became Christians. By today's standards — we often see dozens at Arizona State accept Christ in one week — that seems insignificant. But a foundation was laid for greater future results, and we caught a glimpse of how God could change lives — including ours.

What a miracle! God would use Elmer and me to share His good news in spite of all our imperfections and mistakes. Now we understood what Paul meant when he wrote that ". . . we have this treasure in earthen vessels, that the surpassing greatness of the power may be of God and not from ourselves" (II Corinthians 4:7).

During that year and even the next we saw the ministry get off to a slow but solid start. Yet something was missing, and we couldn't figure out what it was — until we got to Staff Training in Mound, Minn., the summer after our second year on staff.

Chapter 5

A Ministry Mushrooms

I couldn't sleep. It was the last night of Staff Training in August, 1958, and I'd just heard the testimony of Dr. Ralph Byron, world-famous chief surgeon of the City of Hope Hospital in southern California. Now I couldn't get his words out of my mind.

As a medical student, Dr. Byron told us, he'd read the biographies of several great men of God and discovered that they all had one thing in common: They all spent at least one hour alone with God in prayer and Bible study each day. He decided to spend the first hour of every day with God, even though his hospital schedule was such that he got only five hours of sleep most nights.

And God honored that commitment. When he later served in the Marines, Dr. Byron conducted evangelistic meetings and saw hundreds of men become Christians.

I was slowly realizing that I, too, should get up early for a quiet time of prayer and Bible study. As I became painfully aware of how weak my prayer life was, every book or verse I read about prayer made me more and more uncomfortable.

"You know what a sleepy-head I am in the mornings," I argued with the Lord. "It's hard enough for me to get up at all, much less to get up early!"

But various Scriptures kept bombarding my mind — especially the fact that Jesus Himself got up early to pray (Mark 1:35). I stewed a while; then I gave in.

"Okay, Lord. I'll get up for prayer every morning if You'll help me. But I can't do it myself. Please make it impossible for me to go back on this decision."

After that prayer, peace flooded my heart and I slept.

During the next few days it occurred to me that if I, a Christian worker, had a hard time maintaining a consistent quiet time, then some of our students must have the same problem. Maybe we could meet together on campus every morning for devotions.

Early Morning Prayer Meet

I expected to have trouble persuading students to meet me for an early morning quiet time, but it was surprisingly easy. Ten of our students had just returned from a Bible conference and were excited about having devotions together. "It's about time our Christianity cost us something," they said. "If we're going to reach our campus for Christ, we've got to go all-out for God."

We met every week morning from 6:30 to 7 in the campus chapel. I led the group, and as I'd prayed, this made it impossible for me to back out of my commitment. Elmer also believed the prayer group was important, and he babysat in the early mornings so I could lead the group.

For the next seven years groups of students met together for this time of prayer. Every day I prepared devotional sheets that included inspirational quotes, Scripture references and prayer requests for our ministry, for other campuses in Arizona and for other countries. The meeting usually began in silence as we individually had our devotions; then we ended by praying aloud for the day's requests.

As we prayed consistently for discipleship and evangelism on our campus (which was renamed Arizona State University — ASU — in the fall of '58, we prayed for seven categories of students: athletes, blacks, internationals, those in dormitories, fraternities and sororities, and student leaders. We also included requests for special evangelistic meetings.

A Turning Point

Both Elmer and I felt that this prayer emphasis caused a turning point in our ministry. We'd already seen students trust Christ and Christians grow in their faith, but now the ministry snowballed as we saw our prayers answered. Naturally, that excited us even more!

Those involved in the prayer meetings (a nucleus ranging from 10 to 30 students in different years) got excited about their relationships with Christ and became leaders in the ASU ministry. They developed such a strong personal desire to see ASU reached for Christ that they began to share their faith regularly. To do this took real commitment because the only way we knew to teach them how to communicate the gospel was to have them memorize and use the 10-minute presentation, God's Plan.

Ever since we'd come to ASU, Elmer's and my goal was to give each person on campus an opportunity to trust Christ, but the students in the past hadn't believed this was possible and that they could help. As a result, only a few witnessed. Now a grass-roots movement of discipleship and evangelism developed as students individually communicated Christ to others.

A freshman, Sue Rehl, who had become a Christian in high school, talked about Christ with her dorm roommate, Susie Morton. Susie had attended church, but was confused about which religion was true and was searching for answers.

Reaching Women's Dorms

Sue encouraged Susie to talk with me, and she did. As I answered her questions, Susie realized that she first needed to start a personal relationship with Jesus Christ. Then He would give her wisdom to understand the Bible. Susie invited Christ into her life that afternoon.

The next semester, Susie lived with a different roommate, Ginger. As Susie talked with her new roommate about her faith, Ginger trusted Christ and joined Susie in various Christian activities.

Susie and Ginger soon met Barbara Houghton, who lived down the hall from them. They began to spend time with her, taking her with them to evangelistic meetings. Barbara was bitter about life and tried to find happiness in winning campus honors and in having fun. Soon she noticed that Susie and Ginger had peace and an interest in others that she lacked. Ginger brought Barbara to see me, and after I'd shared the gospel with her, she became a Christian, too.

(Left) Elmer, the cook, stands on the left with a buddy at Fort Eustis, Va., in March, 1943. Picture was taken before he became a mess sergeant in charge of preparing daily meals for 600 men at a military prison in Georgia.

(Right) Elmer stands in front of chapel at Camp Stewart, Ga., in June, 1944. Later, he received a medical discharge for rheumatoid arthritis triggered by an army training accident in 1942.

Weekly Campus Crusade staff meetings were held at ASU, like this one in 1975.

On June 1, 1955, the author walked down two aisles. In the morning, she graduated *cum laude* from Bob Jones University, receiving a B.A. in humanities, and that afternoon, she married Elmer in the campus chapel.

The ministry's first student banquet was held in the spring of 1957. Elmer is in the right front with Lee Etta seated next to him and on the left front is Jim Rosscup, the first student chairman.

From left to right, Milt Pope, Elmer's disciple; Elmer; and Dr. Bill Bright, founder and president of Campus Crusade for Christ, in 1959.

The first leadership training classes were held in 1958. Milt Pope operates the projector while Elmer and Lee Etta stand in the background.

In 1960, Elmer (left) and three ASU students gave their testimonies on the radio.

Lee Etta helped Elmer into the car with a patient lift.

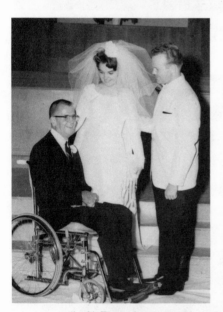

(Left) Elmer Lappen enjoyed performing weddings such as this one on September 10, 1966, for Keith and Verde Geil. Keith, one of Elmer's many converts is now a Methodist minister. (Right) Robert Gurtler and his wife, Alice, shown in the early 1960's. Now known as André Kole, professional illusionist, Bob was challenged by Elmer to join Campus Crusade staff.

Elmer was encouraged by the willingness of faculty members like Dr. George Berkley, associate dean and professor of engineering at ASU, to be involved in the Campus Crusade ministry.

During anti-war protests in the late 1960's, Christian ASU students organized their own demonstration proclaiming that Jesus Christ was the only solution.

This spiritual interest wasn't just limited to the girls' dorms. As Elmer sat at a conference registration table in the student union, an older student came up and said, "My name is Tom Weeks. Tell me about Campus Crusade for Christ and your activities."

They talked for a few minutes, then Tom said, "You'll see a lot more of me."

And we did. Tom had spent several years as an Air Force jet test pilot — and had met Christ through the witness of a fellow officer. When we met him, he was already strong in his faith, and he followed Milt Pope as our ministry's student chairman. He was a backbone of our early morning prayer meetings, daily waking up others and bringing them with him. Two of those he brought were black students, Bob McFadden and Nolan Jones. They enabled us to start a ministry with black students.

'Have You Heard About Nolan?'

Bob was a Christian who was involved in student government with Tom, and Tom encouraged him in his faith. As Bob began to participate in Christian activities, he soon introduced his friend, Nolan, to Christ.

Nolan was a halfback for the campus football team and was well known for kicking extra points. Because everyone at ASU knew who he was, after he became a Christian, his changed life was the talk of the campus: "Have you heard about Nolan Jones? He's stopped going to wild parties and now he talks about God all the time!"

Nolan grew quickly in his faith and soon introduced his girlfriend and a fellow football player to the Lord. Because of the change in Nolan, several black girls became Christians, and I led them in a Bible study. Later, mainly because of Nolan's influence, Elmer and I taught a Bible study that had 25 black men and women in it.

Churches constantly invited Nolan to share his testimony, and he accepted many of these opportunities. He was so eager to mature in his faith that he often stayed at our house late into the night; he was like a sponge, wanting to absorb everything we could teach him about Christ.

After Nolan graduated from ASU, he joined Campus Crusade as its first black staff member. Later he did social work in Ohio and Harlem, where he led many drug addicts to Christ.

As the group prayed, too, for international students, we began to see many of them come to Christ. Nath Gangadean, from the British West Indies, was a skeptic and an intellectual. He attended our evangelistic meetings for several months. One day Elmer challenged him to read the Gospel of John and to pray that God would show him who Jesus Christ really is. Nath accepted the challenge, and after he'd finished the book, he immediately ran across campus to tell us that he'd just received Jesus Christ as Savior and Lord. Nath Gangadean earned a Ph.D. and now teaches world religions at Phoenix College. Every semester he shares his testimony with his classes.

God was also at work in fraternities and sororities. When we had a team meeting at one fraternity, more than half the members expressed an interest in knowing more about Jesus Christ, and the president said, "This is what we need in this fraternity."

After we tried unsuccessfully to set up sorority team meetings, we prayed that at least one sorority girl would become a Christian and have a strong witness in her house. Soon after that the president of Gamma Phi trusted Christ with one of our girls. She grew rapidly in her faith and participated in our ministry's activities.

Reaching Student Leaders

Another of our goals was to see student leaders become Christians. While he was our student chairman, Milt Pope extended this goal. He wanted to infiltrate the student government with Christians because he felt Christians in these positions could best communicate Christ to other student leaders and also influence student government for good. This would in turn be a witness to the entire campus.

During the years our group prayed daily, ASU had five Christian student body presidents in a row. Some were already Christians when they were elected and the others became Christians while in office. One of these student body presidents, Karl Dennison, was a Christian involved in our ministry who was elected as a result of our specific prayers.

In fact, it was the urging of other Christian students that first persuaded Karl to run for student body president. They prayed for him daily throughout the election, and several helped campaign for him. Often during the election Karl insisted, "I know that, if it's God's will, I'll be elected." For a while his chances of winning looked bleak because the powerful fraternity "machine" solidly backed his opponent. Yet Karl was elected by an overwhelming majority of votes.

Other Christians took leadership positions, including the president of Associated Women Students, a dorm president and the chief justice of the student court (who later became an Arizona state senator).

One year Tom Weeks was in charge of a campus weekend student leaders' workshop. Traditionally, on Friday and Saturday night of the workshop, most of the participants went to a local bar. Tom was concerned that this not happen while he was in charge, and asked others to pray to that end. He also planned a busy workshop schedule, including recreation.

But during the weekend, some put pressure on Tom to let them go to the bar. Tom stood his ground and insisted that they follow the schedule. If they didn't he would resign as their leader. Most of the 100 students cooperated, and at the end of the workshop, they even elected Tom the outstanding leader of the weekend.

Those active in our prayer time also prayed for every Campus Crusade meeting we had, sometimes even forming special prayer chains, and we saw exciting results. We planned to show a specific film at an evangelistic meeting in which we wanted to see God work in a special way. We asked students to pray during the first minute of every hour on the day of the meeting. Several students did this, claiming Scripture promises.

The Largest Meeting

They also prayed that specific people would attend the meeting; then they invited them to come. That night we were thrilled to see 123 people at the meeting, including many of those we'd prayed for. That was the largest evangelistic meeting we'd had. Best of all, five people trusted Christ that night, and several others indicated an interest in hearing more.

Our ministry grew so much that in fall of 1960 Campus Crusade assigned three more staff members to join Elmer and me at ASU. One of them was a single woman that I trained to take my place since I was expecting a second child early in 1961. (Our daughter, Beverly Joy, was born the following January.)

The larger ministry also created a need for new facilities. We had a weekly meeting called Leadership Training Class (LTC) to train our students in methods of evangelism and discipleship. One night, when some of our local Campus Crusade advisory board members noticed that more than 40 students were packed into our tiny living room, they suggested that we get a bigger home.

Several of the board members thought the board should help us get a new house. One of them, Elmer Bradley, even drew up blueprints and took us to look at model homes. But as the ASU staff and board members asked God for larger facilities, we received no definite answer.

More than a year passed, and we still hadn't reached a decision. Finally board chairman Arlis Priest called a special meeting to vote on building a Campus Crusade house.

The night before the meeting, a board member and his wife came over to pray with Elmer and me about getting the house. As we prayed, the man said, "Where is the verse that says, 'I, being in the way, the Lord led me'? We need to pray for the Lord to lead us."

"That's Genesis 24:27," Elmer said.

'Room for the Camels'

I looked it up and as I did, I noticed verse 31 of the same chapter. Then I read it aloud: "Come in, thou blessed of the

Lord; wherefore standest thou without? For I have prepared the house, and room for the camels" (King James
Version).

All four of us burst into laughter. We knew that this
verse is part of a passage in which Abraham had sent his
servant to seek a Canaanite wife for his son, Isaac, and
God led the servant to Rebekah. In Genesis 24:31, Rebekah's brother, Laban, is extending hospitality to the servant.

Yet we felt that God was inviting us to move into a new
house that He was about to provide — a house that had
"room for the camels." (In our case, this meant room for the
college students we were ministering to.) The next day the
board voted to build the house and soon purchased a corner
lot on Broadway Avenue, one of the busiest thoroughfares
in Tempe. In January, 1963, we moved into our new house.

Even though we were ministering to larger groups of
students, we never forgot the importance of building individuals in their faith. In fact, we spent most of our time
with individuals who had a strong desire to grow spiritually. Through emphasizing personal evangelism, prayer,
Bible study and memorization, and being filled with the
Holy Spirit, we helped them to mature. In addition, we
challenged them to develop leadership by continually giving them more responsibilities in the ASU ministry.

After these men and women developed daily personal
walks with God, we encouraged them to teach other students the things we'd taught them.

This discipleship caused our ministry to grow still
more. By now the ministry seemed to be going so well that
we couldn't even imagine what else God would do to expand and bless it. What could possibly come next?

Chapter 6

Branching Out

When speech teacher Margaret Jane Rice received a list of speakers for ASU's annual Spiritual Exploration Week, she promptly tossed it into her wastebasket. During that week various campus religious groups always offered special speakers, and teachers had the option of inviting them to speak in their classes. However, these speakers were notoriously boring.

Later Mrs. Rice decided she should at least look over the list, so she dug it out of the trash. As she scanned it, she noticed that John Flack, a speaker for Campus Crusade, had listed 25 subjects that he could speak on. Mrs. Rice had never heard of either the speaker or the organization, but the fact that he'd listed so many different topics intrigued her. She thought the talk called "What Makes People Like You?" might be good for her freshman speech students, so she decided to invite John to speak to them.

Fake Titles

She didn't know then that most of John's topics were fake titles he'd written to amuse Elmer, me and the rest of the staff. He'd expected us to catch the joke, then submit only the serious titles to the Spiritual Emphasis Week publicity committee. When John, a traveling representative for Campus Crusade, arrived at ASU, he was horrified that his joke had been taken seriously and that titles like "Great Men Who Have Known Me" and "What's the Big Idea" (discussing the philosophies of Kant, Nietzsche, Freud and Christ) had been circulated all over campus. In fact, his talk for Mrs. Rice's class was one of the joke titles, so he frantically wrote a message on qualities for popularity that stressed the importance of a personal relationship with Jesus Christ.

At the end of John's first talk in her class, Mrs. Rice asked, "For the benefit of any interested students, would you tell us how a person can become a Christian if he wants to?" (Usually Campus Crusade staff who speak in classes ask those who are interested in knowing Christ to indicate this on comment cards. Then staff or students visit them and personally share the gospel with them.)

Although she thought she was already a Christian, Mrs. Rice listened carefully as John explained how to start a personal relationship with Jesus Christ. He told the class that God loves them and offers a wonderful plan for their lives, but that man is sinful and separated from God, which prevents him from experiencing this love and plan. He continued that Jesus Christ is God's only provision for man's sin, and that, to become a Christian, one must individually receive Jesus Christ as Savior and Lord. He ended by saying that a person can do this by prayer, asking Christ to come into his life. He suggested that those interested read the Gospel of John three times, saying, "This was meant for me."

The next day John spoke to another of Mrs. Rice's classes. Again she made the same request at the end of his talk. John was puzzled. "You asked that question yesterday, didn't you?"

"Yes, I did," she explained. "But this is a different group of students, and I want them to know, too. By the way, I'm reading the book of John."

Guess Who?

That night Mrs. Rice and her husband had dinner at the Sigma Chi house, and who should speak after dinner but John Flack! By this time it had dawned on Mrs. Rice that she didn't actually have a personal relationship with Christ although she was an active church member.

The next day John and another Campus Crusade staff member, Sharon Carlson, went to Mrs. Rice's office. "We're not only here on campus to help students, but we're also here for the faculty," John said. Then he and Sharon explained the gospel once again, and Mrs. Rice asked Christ to come into her life.

Sharon followed up Mrs. Rice, teaching her basic principles about the Christian life. She introduced her to me, and I began to meet with her for prayer and Bible study.

This study later grew to include a group of faculty women. Mrs. Rice was so excited about her new faith that she shared the good news with everyone. As a speech teacher, she presented her testimony in a clear, dynamic way and was invited often to speak in churches and Christian Women's Clubs.

Mrs. Rice was the first of several faculty members we've worked with. In fact, as we've ministered to students. the lives of faculty and people in the community have also been touched. We've helped them to grow in their faith, involving them in our ministry with students. As a result, several of these lay people have developed outstanding ministries of their own.

Laymen

Carl Heath was a committed Christian who was active in his church. A busy high school science teacher, counselor and basketball coach, he used his spare time to help people, teaching Sunday school and doing volunteer work in hospitals. But Carl had never seen anybody trust Christ through his ministry.

A friend suggested that Carl attend a training class we were starting for laymen that was similar to LTC, and he did. As a result of learning how to be filled with the Holy Spirit and how to witness, Carl's ministry changed dramatically.

Choking Heart and Sweaty Palms

Yet the technique Carl used in his first witnessing experience left something to be desired. Elmer had asked him to write down his testimony and share it with someone. He did so, choosing to talk with one of his players while the two drove to a meeting. "I shared my testimony with him and then, in the worst salesmanship in the world, I said, 'John, you wouldn't like to invite Christ into your life, would you?'" Carl recalled. "My heart was choking me and my palms were hot and sweaty. John blurted out, 'I sure would!' I pulled the car over to the side of the road, and he followed me in the sinner's prayer. A few years later I was invited to his ordination as a minister."

Carl's technique in witnessing soon improved, and he took advantage of his school and church contacts to tell those around him how they could meet Christ. Many times he phoned Elmer, saying, "I thought you'd like to know that two studetns received Christ with me in my office about half an hour ago. I won't keep you; I know you're busy. God bless you!"

Carl, who no longer teaches, has seen more than 400 people become Christians through his ministry and more than 25 of these now serve Christ full time. One of them was his friend Don Orvis.

Don taught math and was a basketball referee in the same school system as Carl. Late on Monday night Don saw Carl in Guggy's Restaurant, and he asked, "How does the season look, coach? How many games do you think you'll win?"

"I think we'll do pretty well," Carl predicted. "Say, Don, I've been wanting to see you. There's something I want to share with you about God's love."

Don gulped, thinking, "Let me out of here." Then he tried to change the subject back to basketball. But Carl lovingly persisted in talking about spiritual things, aided by Don's roommate, who was also a Christian. "When could we get together to talk about it?" Carl asked Don.

"Let's make an appointment right now," Don's roommate chimed in. Don agreed to an appointment on the following Thursday, but wasn't at all sure he really wanted to.

Sensing Emptiness

During the next few days Don began to sense an emptiness in his life that his usual pursuit of fun couldn't fill. He began to wonder if there was more to life and if indeed God could make the difference that Carl thought He could. Now he looked forward to the talk with Carl.

As Don went into the church where he was to meet Carl on Thursday, a girl he knew was leaving. "Are you going to talk to Coach Heath?" she greeted him. "You'll like what he tells you! He just told me how I could know God personally."

"Wait here," Don answered. "I'll be out in a little while." She stayed, then a half hour later Don joined her. They left together, both bubbling over about their new relationships with God.

Soon after this, a Campus Crusade traveling representative spoke at Don's church, and Don picked her up at the airport. When he told her he was a new Christian, she urged him to look up Elmer and to attend our LTC classes.

Don showed up at the next class meeting, which was a training session on witnessing. Eager to try it himself, he phoned Elmer the next day and said, "I'm coming to pick you up, and we're going out witnessing together." They arranged to go to ASU during Don's free time later in the morning. Soon Elmer and Don began to share their faith together daily, and Elmer discipled Don.

'I'll Throw You In'

In addition to his time with Elmer, Don spent the rest of his free time ministering. Every night he was either involved in church activities, witnessing at Williams Air Force Base or at an ASU dorm. A year later, in response to a challenge from Elmer, Don gave up some of his ASU activities to begin a ministry at newly opened Mesa Community College.

Elmer asked Don to be the chairman of our annual evangelistic Christmas party in 1965, and Don took on this responsibility, too. "We're going to have 1,000 people at that party," Don half-seriously kidded.

"Don, the very most that hall at Holiday Village will hold is 500," Elmer corrected him. "We're not going to have 1,000; we wouldn't know what to do with that many."

"If 1,000 do come, I'm going to throw you in the swimming pool," Don threatened.

Although we didn't have 1,000 people at our Christmas party, the crowd was still the largest we'd ever had — 500 students and laymen. That night 30 people indicated that they'd trusted Christ at the party, and of these, eight eventually entered full-time Christian work.

At the end of the school year, Don resigned his teaching job to attend Denver Conservative Baptist Theological

Seminary. Working toward two graduate degrees kept him busy, but he still spent much time in discipleship and evangelism. He began a student ministry in Denver similar to ours and encouraged the seminary students to work with him. After graduation, the seminary invited him to join its staff as professor of evangelism, a position in which he still serves.

Living Scripture

Don recently recalled the impact Elmer's example had on him. "I have taken theology courses; I am a theological professor," he said, "and I have seen students memorize Scripture for classes. But Elmer had the Scripture living inside, and it flowed. The first summer I knew him, he caused me to memorize more than 200 verses and never once told me to do it. I just saw it flowing and said, 'I want to be like that.' "

We rejoiced to see God build people like Don through our ministry. During the 1960's we saw hundreds receive Christ and begin to mature in Him. But to make the most of this spiritual harvest, we had to pack days that were already full with even more ministry activities.

During this time, Elmer gradually experienced more and more pain from arthritis. It became agony just to walk. The heavy load of ministry activities intensified his physical problems; but he didn't want to give up anything he was doing. Instead he kept on going.

We went to various doctors in hopes that different treatments would ease Elmer's pain. Yet nothing seemed to help. Elmer's condition got even worse.

In summer, 1964, we went to an arthritis clinic in Oregon for a few weeks. The doctors there advised Elmer to gradually stop taking cortisone because they were beginning to find that it often caused dangerous side effects.

To help Elmer break his physical dependence on cortisone, he occasionally had to take special booster shots of ACTH (a form of cortisone). At first, going to the doctor's office for a shot was routine. But by fall, it became a nightmare. It was so painful for Elmer to get in and out of cars that the nurse came out to the car to give him his shot.

By October the pain intensified to the point that Elmer felt walking was more agonizing than it was worth. One morning, after he'd struggled several minutes to get out of the shower, Elmer headed for bed instead of campus. "This is it," he thought to himself. "I just can't take any more of this."

Chapter 7

Testing, One, Two, Three . . .

Trying to continue his active ministry as long as he could, Elmer had fought his arthritis and stayed on his feet. Now he experienced so much pain and weakness that he had to lay aside his ministry to rest and get his strength back.

This would probably take three months, Elmer estimated. The ASU staff team could keep the ministry running until he was well enough to participate actively again.

Instead of feeling that his ministry had suddenly been snatched away, Elmer once again chose to trust God with his physical condition and to see what would happen next.

"I didn't feel like I'd been taken to a cliff and dropped off," Elmer recalled. "Remember, I'd already spent four years in the hospital with arthritis. What was new about being out three months? I remembered that 'the *steps* of a good man are ordered by the Lord . . .' (Psalm 37:23a, King James Version), and I realized, so are the *stops*."

Although Elmer was too weak at first to do much more than sleep, within a few weeks he began to direct the ministry from his bed. Twice a week he met with his staff team to find out what was happening on campus and to tell them what they needed to do in the following days. Elmer also spent time saturating his mind with the Word of God and planning future ministry events. Still, he needed to rest most of the time.

Elmer's prediction was wrong; his confinement lasted for nearly a year. And because he lacked strength, he was unable to minister full time for almost two years. He didn't know then that he'd never walk again. He would return to his responsibilities in a wheelchair.

Extra Grace

Even though the 1964-65 school year was especially painful, God gave Elmer an extra measure of grace to keep an incredibly positive attitude. But in many ways my responses were far from joyful, and it was harder for me to learn to trust God with the negative circumstances we faced.

At first it wasn't difficult to deal with Elmer's worsened physical condition and the changes that coping with it made in our family. Practically everyone we knew was praying for us, and their love and prayers protected us like a blanket.

Gradually that sense of protection wore off, although people were still praying and expressing their love. I loved Elmer so much that I wanted to do everything I could for him during this illness. This meant staying home with him, being available to help him 24 hours a day. Because he was confined to home, so was I.

Yet as weeks stretched into months, I got tired of staying home. I'm naturally independent, liking the freedom to do things on my own. Now my freedom had been taken away from me, and I resented it.

I felt trapped because I couldn't leave Elmer for more than an hour at a time. Rarely could I go out to lunch or attend a Christian Women's Club meeting.

Along with feeling trapped, I felt guilty. Elmer was helpless and in pain. Physically, he was forced to depend on me to take care of him. He didn't like being the cause of my confinement any more than I liked losing my freedom.

I found myself expressing my resentment through the way I did my household chores. I cooked meals because I had to, but I didn't go out of my way to make them interesting. A simple thing like doing the breakfast dishes became a big chore to me.

Draining Chores

Not only did I resent having to stay home all the time, but my responsibilities there were physically demanding. In addition to doing housework and caring for three children, I was now a full-time nurse. I had to bathe and dress Elmer daily, prepare and bring him meals. To keep him from getting bedsores, I had to turn him over in bed several times a day and night.

A doctor told Elmer to drink two quarts of raw vegetable juice every day. For almost nine months, I spent a large chunk of every day making this awful-tasting drink, which contained the juices of carrots, potatoes, celery and cucumbers.

I had to work hard to do all these tasks, and it wore me out physically. For almost two years, until Elmer was able to handle a normal level of activity, this was my daily life.

God wanted to teach me how to be a servant — a necessary part of any Christian's ministry. But I didn't learn these lessons on servanthood willingly. During the year Elmer was bedfast, I'd taken over leadership of a weekly training class for lay people that Elmer had started that fall. This class, which met for one hour a week in our college room, and the campus ministry had showed me how fulfilling it could be to have a public ministry.

But the next year, as Elmer began to get stronger, I had to devote full time to taking Elmer places for his ministry. I no longer had time for a ministry of my own, and I resented it.

'Nothing But A Slave'

"Lord, you've forgotten me!" I complained. "You've stuck me in this corner, and I'm nothing but a slave!"

At that time I thought I was more important when I was teaching a class on being filled with the Holy Spirit or sharing Christ with someone than I was when I was making vegetable juice or taking Elmer someplace. All this resentment made it doubly hard to get my work done because it drained my strength even more than the hard work did.

When it became obvious, in 1965, that Elmer wasn't going to walk again, I began to feel disillusioned. For the last four years I'd prayed for a miracle — that God would somehow heal Elmer completely. I expected his healing so much that I began to look for it around every corner. But Elmer was too weak to walk again.

Because of my resentment toward my circumstances and my disillusionment that Elmer hadn't been healed, it was hard for me to pray or read the Bible. Also, I had a hard time witnessing or talking with people about anything.

Gradually I recognized that my resentment and disillusionment were sin. The circumstances Elmer and I were facing *were* hard. But God wanted me to trust Him to sustain me, as Elmer was. Instead of carrying burdens that God never intended me to struggle with, He wanted me to cast them on Him. God wanted me to believe that He'd somehow bring good out of this calamity.

Blessings and Encouragement

Nothing dramatic happened to change my wrong attitudes. Rather, my convictions about prayer motivated me to change. In the past I'd said that prayer was a priority, and that evangelism and discipleship suffered if they weren't backed by prayer. If I really believed this, then my ministry wasn't cut off even though I couldn't spend time on campus. I could still have a ministry of prayer as I worked at home. And before I could effectively pray, I had to confess my sin, restoring my fellowship with God.

After I began to act on these conclusions, it became much easier to do everything I had to do. My difficult circumstances hadn't changed at all, but my response to them had, and that made a world of difference in my ability to cope.

Even though these two years were extremely hard, God gave Elmer and me various blessings along the way for encouragement. I loved leading the weekly laymen's training classes during the 1964-65 school year. Each class ran for seven sessions, and we began a new cycle as soon as one ended. That year we trained 500 lay people from the Phoenix area.

The only way to explain the success of that class is that it was the result of an incredible working of God's Spirit. It began because some laymen who wanted to learn to share their faith asked us for training. I never promoted the lay training class because I didn't have time. Yet the attendance was overwhelming — the Holy Spirit just drew people there as class members told their friends!

Sustaining Friends

The love shown by friends and acquaintances also encouraged us. Many people prayed daily for Elmer and wrote him frequent letters. Some ran errands for us. A man in our lay class who was a barber came to our house to cut Elmer's hair. Later, when Elmer was taking special hot bath therapy, laymen and students often took Elmer to a heated swimming pool. Bill Bright phoned from time to time, expressing his concern for what we faced and his encouragement to persevere.

One friend, Bobbie Taylor, was especially encouraging. We prayed together on the phone at least weekly and sometimes daily — and still do.

Though all three of our children have always been special blessings to us, it was particularly true now. (Our third child, Steve, had been born in April, 1964.) When Elmer became bedfast, Steve was only six months old. You might think it was a terrible burden to take care of a baby when your husband had a prolonged illness. Actually we felt he was a gift from the Lord; he took our minds off our problems and was entertaining. Because Elmer and I were at home all the time, we had more time to watch his growth than we'd had to watch Jon's or Bev's. (Jon was now eight and Bev was three and a half.) It was fun to have a baby around the house!

Even though they were so young, Jon and Bev helped me with many household chores. They picked up their toys, dusted furniture, washed dishes, watched the baby and got things for Elmer. Jon ran errands and helped Elmer get dressed. We had to work as a unit, sharing the chores, and this responsibility probably made our children more independent, able to do things by their own initiative. I think every family needs to share chores, but our family *had* to pull together to survive.

A Special Friend

His friendship with Don Orvis was a special joy to Elmer. They met in spring, 1965, after Elmer was strong enough to leave the house occasionally. Don was a new Christian then, and he wanted to witness on campus with

Elmer. To do this, Don had to come to our house, pick up Elmer and put him in his car. Once they got to campus, Don put Elmer in his wheelchair and pushed him to the social sciences building. This became a daily routine. (Later we got a patient lift — a machine we used to hoist Elmer from his wheelchair into a car or into bed.)

Don and Elmer became close friends, spending a lot of time together outside their witnessing sessions. When Elmer began to take daily hot water therapy, Don either took him to a heated pool or lined up others to do it. The hot water therapy relaxed Elmer, and he used the time to disciple Don. Often they memorized Scripture together or Elmer taught Don principles on walking with God. These times were refreshing to both men.

The following year, as he was able to spend more time on campus, Elmer asked God to give him a group of 12 young men to disciple. He'd been impressed by the fact that Jesus had worked closely with 12 men during the three years of His public ministry. Working with a group would be the best use of Elmer's strength, and it would expand his ministry.

God more than amply answered Elmer's prayer — He gave him a group of 13 men, most of whom were in Lambda Chi fraternity. Elmer met with the group once a week for Bible study, Scripture memorization and prayer. He also spent time individually with each member, witnessing or meeting personal needs. All of these men grew strong in their walks with God. Later all 13 entered full-time Christian work.

Unexpected Blessing

As Elmer grew stronger, we found that his pain didn't end. He tried three main types of therapy during this time — drinking raw vegetable juice, physical therapy and the hot water treatments. None of these cured him, but the nutritional approach brought an unexpected blessing.

Elmer had several knots caused by calcium deposits that gnarled arthritic joints in his feet, legs and hands. During the hospitalization just before Elmer entered Bob

Jones University, his right leg became permanently immovable. His doctor put it in a cast to straighten it, allowing him to walk. For years, there'd been a calcium deposit as big as a walnut on the left side of his knee.

After Elmer had been drinking the vegetable juice for a few months, we suddenly noticed that this calcium deposit had dissolved; Elmer could bend his right leg for the first time in years! That turned out to be a real bonus because being able to bend both legs allowed Elmer to sit comfortably in a wheelchair. We felt this was God's way of preparing Elmer for life in a wheelchair.

Although he obviously preferred to walk — and to walk normally — in some ways Elmer had less pain now that he was in a wheelchair. When he walked he was carrying his weight on already painful feet and legs, causing them to hurt even more. Also, the twists he had to make to compensate for his stiff leg further strained him. He could avoid all that by sitting in a wheelchair, being lifted and lowered by others.

Ministering From A Wheelchair

Using his wheelchair freed Elmer to use his limited strength for ministry, rather than exhausting himself in getting around. Yet he had to make several adjustments to minister from a wheelchair, and these were hard for him.

Elmer was a disciplined person by nature, thriving on making the most of his time and accomplishing goals that he set for himself. Planning was a vital part of this discipline. But we discovered that a person in a wheelchair has to think everything through in advance just to survive.

When he took his disciples out to share Christ on campus, Elmer encouraged them to set up appointments in advance. If they didn't have appointments, they approached people at random who were sitting by sidewalks or on the ground floors of buildings. Being in a wheelchair restricted Elmer's movements on campus. He had to find new places to talk to people because some of his favorite spots couldn't be reached by wheelchair.

Now Elmer couldn't go with our staff to the dorms one night a week to make appointments to share the gospel.

Steps became a barrier that he avoided whenever possible
— it took several men to carry his wheelchair up them. To
meet with students outside, Elmer had to pick firm, flat
places where his wheelchair wouldn't tip over.

Since Elmer had already been unable to drive, he was
used to finding people to drive him places. Now that he
couldn't walk, he also had to arrange for someone to push
his wheelchair when he reached his destination.

Getting places took longer because Elmer had to allow
time to be lifted in and out of the car. This forced him to cut
down the number of activities he participated in since it
took longer to do everything. At times this frustrated
Elmer.

Making Adjustments

To save unnecessary steps for others, he learned to plan
the materials he needed for every activity and to take
them with him. We also learned to set things within
Elmer's limited reach — especially when he was working
alone. If someone walked off with Elmer's only pen at a
time when he needed to write, Elmer got frustrated.

During his Army days, Elmer had learned that,
whenever possible, an effective leader joins his followers
in doing the tasks he's asked them to do. This sets the pace
for his men and increases their morale. Leading by example had become a natural part of Elmer's life. Now he
missed being able to physically lead his staff, students and
family.

It was hard for Elmer to depend on others to get places.
He liked to be early or on time for appointments.
Whenever anyone didn't pick him up on time, he was late.
If someone didn't show up to take him somewhere, Elmer
missed his appointments.

"This is still one of the biggest problems I have to face,"
Elmer said years later. "But that's the way it is, and I've
learned to accept being dependent on others." To prevent
misunderstandings, he double-checked all his plans, encouraging those around him to be punctual or early for
appointments.

Enhanced Discipleship

In spite of all the hardships, struggles and adjustments we had to make between fall, 1964, and fall, 1966, we saw God bring good out of seeming disaster. God showed Himself powerful to resolve all our problems in response to our trust.

One blessing of not being able to minister directly on campus for several months was that Elmer learned how much his staff could accomplish. God's Spirit and the staff's hard work caused the ministry to flourish during 1964-66. Elmer learned to appreciate their work more, realizing that the ministry could go on without him.

His restriction to a wheelchair created opportunities to disciple others. Since he almost always needed people with him, he used the time to encourage their spiritual growth. Physically, Elmer was forced to follow the basic principle of discipleship, "Never do anything alone. Always take someone with you to do evangelism or follow-up." This became so essential to Elmer's ministry that later he turned down a gift of money for a motorized wheelchair.

Often Elmer would memorize Scripture with his disciples or discuss some area of the Christian life with them. He also motivated his men to action. As they went to campus, perhaps he'd ask a disciple, "Dick, what are you going to do with your life after you graduate from ASU?"

"I think God's calling me to be a pastor," Dick might answer.

"That's great! Have you checked out seminaries yet to see where God would have you go?"

"No . . ."

"I'll tell you what: Why don't you write off for some catalogs? In a couple of weeks when you get them, we can talk about how to choose the right seminary."

And Dick could be sure that Elmer would remember to check in a few days to see if he'd sent away for his catalogs.

Elmer never used his handicap as an excuse not to keep active in his ministry. In spite of his limitations, Elmer worked as hard as he ever had and never felt sorry for himself.

"I'm not going to live every day feeling like I have to be healed," Elmer declared. "I'd welcome healing — who wouldn't? — but I *refuse* to believe that God can't use me like I am. I'd challenge anybody who thinks differently."

By the grace of God, Elmer and I weathered hard times those two years. But our lives and ministries weren't exactly rosy after that. Instead, we realized that we had an enemy. And that enemy tried to discourage us, sabotage our work and attack us every way he could. He was out to destroy us.

Chapter 8

Blitz and Blessing

No wonder our enemy — Satan — wanted to destroy us. The ministry was going even better than ever. During this time, our evangelistic meetings began to be especially fruitful.

In 1970, Elmer conducted a meeting with the ASU football team that we considered the best team meeting we'd ever seen. To our amazement, the head coach made attendance at our meeting mandatory for all 92 players and six coaches. Most of them weren't too thrilled about it, but they gathered before practice one fall Wednesday on a section of bleachers in Sun Devil Stadium.

The meeting started with a bang; the assistant coach who introduced our student emcee bungled the Campus Crusade name. Then the emcee, while sharing a little of his testimony, gave the impression that his walk with God had caused him to lose all interest in girls. The whole team roared at this because it confirmed their stereotype that Christianity was for sissies. Elmer, the main speaker, had to follow these mistakes. How could he get the team's attention now?

Elmer told the Sun Devils about his own special love for sports, saying that he considered it a privilege to talk to them. "I'd really like to get close to you guys," he said. "David Buchanan, where are you? Stand up."

David, the left halfback, reluctantly stood as everyone looked at him. He knew what was coming.

"David, you and I got real close last Saturday night. When you ran out of bounds you put your foot right on the left part of my wheelchair." (Elmer had sat on the sidelines of the field.) David sank down, embarrassed, as his teammates snickered.

"Men," Elmer continued, "in 1954 UCLA was the number one college team in the nation. Eight of 11 starting players on that team had their faith in Christ. That's what counts; that's what's going to last when the glory of being on a top team is only a memory.

A Has-been

"Look at me; I played ball in high school. Now I'm a has-been. And that's what you're going to be someday, too."

Now the whole team was hooked. Elmer proceeded to explain God's Plan. As a result, 61 out of 92 players responded positively to Elmer's challenge. Some received Christ; some wanted to learn how to grow spiritually; and others wanted more information about Christianity. To say the least, follow-up was hectic.

Two years later we witnessed a still greater response to the gospel. André Kole, a Campus Crusade staff member who uses magical illusions to present spiritual truth, performed at ASU. He did two shows at Grady Gammage Auditorium, the largest auditorium in the area, and more than 5,000 attended. Of these, more than 830 indicated that they'd received Christ that evening, and 900 others were interested in getting more information about a relationship with God.

We'd prayed that 1,000 people would become Christians through this special event. As our staff and students followed up those who'd responded positively, we saw well over that number trust Christ.

Our Christian students developed a bolder witness during the late 1960's in response to a free speech movement among college students throughout the nation. In 1970, we organized our LTC students to witness by a "divide and conquer" method. They met as a group for instructions and prayer, broke up into pairs to share their faith, then gathered to tell how God had used them. We did this every week, with groups that ranged from 12 to 100.

'We'd Better Pray'

Along with the free speech movement came student protests and demonstrations against the Vietnamese war. During one demonstration, some of our students organized their own demonstration. They carried signs like "End the War in Your Heart" and told students how they could do this through a relationship with Jesus Christ.

After four students were killed at Kent State University during anti-war demonstrations that spring, some students at ASU organized a protest against the government's handling of the incident. A group of students carried signs, boycotted classes and tried to keep other students and faculty from getting to class. Campus officials feared that the unrest was going to get worse.

Later that day a dean invited Elmer to come to his office and talk with him about the problem. "I'm very concerned about the atmosphere on campus right now," the dean told Elmer. "Would you have a special prayer meeting about it? You can also tell your students that my office will be open all day tomorrow to anyone who wants to come in and pray with me."

That night 30 students joined us at the campus chapel to pray for peace on campus. The next day several students went to the dean's office to pray. "We'd *better* pray," the dean told them, "there's no other answer to this."

That day the climate on campus changed. The protest never peaked to a frenzy as the faculty feared it would. Instead, the demonstrators calmed down and let the campus get back to normal. We praised God that He'd answered our prayers so quickly.

We'd already learned that, as we moved out for the Lord, we could expect spiritual warfare. Someone has said that you can't move without producing friction. That's true! Whenever God was about to use one of our projects in a big way, Satan would try to keep it from happening.

Probably the biggest attack we ever experienced was during preparation for EXPLO '72. EXPLO was a week-long conference held in Dallas during June of 1972 that trained more than 80,000 Christians in how to share their faith. We'd already recruited special prayer groups all over Arizona to pray for EXPLO. Our goal was for 1,000 Arizona students and laymen to attend. In March, we'd planned to launch an all-out campaign to publicize the

conference. Our staff would show a promotional film and
speak at every church, student and civic group they could.
We also handed out brochures on campus.

Jon Runs Away

Just before this campaign began, our 15-year-old son,
Jon, ran away. We were convinced that Jon's disappearance was Satan's way of stopping our all-important
EXPLO promotion because of the timing. He was trying to
divert us from working on our campaign by causing us to
focus all our attention on Jon. Because we could expect
him to open fire against our ministry, Satan ambushed our
family instead — a more vulnerable spot where we weren't
expecting attack.

One night Jon announced, "I can't stand school another
minute! Let me drop out for the rest of the year and take a
vacation."

Elmer and I were horrified. We knew Jon had had
trouble adjusting to school that year, but we were scared
that if he dropped out, he'd never finish high school.

"Jon, you can't drop out of school now," we reasoned
with him. "It would be like suicide for a young person to
drop out during his second year of high school. You need
your education to survive in today's world. Can't you hang
on till summer vacation? That's not even three months
from now."

"No, I need a vacation *now*," he insisted. We didn't
know that he was under a lot of pressure. He'd cut classes
with his friends so often that it would be almost impossible
for him to catch up on all the work he'd missed. Apparently, Jon's school didn't keep very good attendance re-
cords that year, and no one from the school ever notified us
that he was cutting classes.

The next afternoon Jon didn't come home after school.
This didn't bother me because I thought he'd probably
gone to a friend's house. But when he wasn't back for
supper, I began to wonder where he was. He usually called
if he was going to miss a meal. We knew something was
wrong later that evening when he still wasn't home.

We figured Jon was probably mad at us because we wouldn't let him leave school and that he was probably staying with a friend. Surely he'd call us later that night or the next morning to let us know where he was.

Two days went by with no sign of Jon, and we were worried. We didn't know what to do, so we called the police to tell them Jon was missing. The police immediately assumed that Jon had run away, although it took us a few days to realize that really was what had happened.

Attack on Our Family

I've never experienced anything that made me as anxious as Jon's disappearance. How could he make it on his own? As I looked around his room, I couldn't see anything missing; he hadn't taken money, clothes or even a sleeping bag.

I don't know why I didn't think of it sooner, but on the fifth day I looked under Jon's pillow. There I found a note saying that he'd run away, not to worry and not to call the police. He explained that he was sick of the hassles at school and that he just had to get away.

For the first several days after Jon ran away, we didn't tell any of the other staff about it. We didn't think Jon would be gone long and everything would be settled soon. We did everything we normally did. But we finally realized that we should share what we were going through, that Jon might not come home for a while. During a staff meeting Elmer reluctantly told our staff team that Jon had run away, nearly breaking down as he did so. They prayed with us for Jon's safe return, also putting the request on our special EXPLO 24-hour prayer chain.

A few days later we got a letter from Jon. He said he'd found a job taking care of animals on a ranch. He told us he was all right and that we shouldn't worry. There was no return address or postmark on the letter to tell us where he was.

We prayed harder than ever, and I fasted for five days. We felt the whole episode was an attack of Satan on our

family to try to stop our ministry. It seemed as though
Satan had dropped a bomb on us to keep us from promoting
EXPLO '72.

A Defeated Enemy

During this time I was teaching a Bible study on Ephesians at our intermediate LTC, and we were discussing our
"throne rights" over Satan. These truths sustained me
during this time, encouraging me to pray with assurance
for Jon's safe return and for the success of our EXPLO
promotion.

In the Bible study, we discussed how we can claim
victory over Satan because Jesus Christ defeated him
through His death on the cross. According to I John 3:8b,
"The Son of God appeared for this purpose, that He might
destroy the works of the devil." The works of the devil are
sin and death. Through His death and resurrection, Christ
rendered "powerless him who has the power of death, that
is, the devil" (Hebrews 2:14b).

Not only is Satan a defeated enemy, but Jesus Christ is
seated at the right hand of God the Father (Ephesians
1:20-22). He is "far above all rule and authority and power
and dominion, and every name that is named." God also
"put *all things in subjection under His feet*" (italics mine).
When we come to know Christ, we are raised up with Him,
and seated with Him in the heavenly places (Ephesians
2:6).

Because of these truths, we can't let Satan bluff us by
claiming victory over us that he doesn't actually have.
He's a strong enemy, but he has only as much power as God
allows him to have (see Job 1:7-12). Satan knows that God
is in control and that his time to have power over mankind
is limited (Revelation 12:10-12).

We must claim in prayer the fact that God, who is in
us, is greater than Satan, who is in the world (I John 4:4).
We're fighting a spiritual battle in which God *commands*
us to be strong in Him and in His strength, and to put on
God's armor so we can stand firm against Satan's schemes
(Ephesians 6:10-17). Because Christ has overcome Satan,
we have guaranteed victory; if we resist the devil, he *will*

flee from us (James 4:7). But first we must resist him by being aware of what he's doing and claiming the fact that Christ has already won the victory.

Although we worried about Jon at times, we also prayed fervently for him on the basis of our throne rights over Satan. "Lord, thank You that You know where Jon is and that You're taking care of him. Thank You that You're in control of what happens to him and that Satan has no power over Jon. Please bring Jon back to us quickly."

Jon Returns

Before long we saw our prayers answered and the attack on our family fell apart. Jon came home three weeks after he ran away.

He was still rebellious, but our communication was better than it had been before. Working on a ranch that didn't have modern plumbing or other things that we take for granted caused Jon to appreciate his home more. He'd missed so much school that he had to drop out for the rest of the semester after all. He got a job in a car wash, also taking a correspondence course. Fortunately, his time away from school was only temporary. He finished high school and later went to college for two years before joining the Navy.

And Satan's intended sabotage of our EXPLO promotion failed. We were told later that the Arizona delegation of 1,500 was the second largest group at the conference.

After EXPLO '72, we saw that Satan also attacks in subtler ways. He tries to discourage us when conditions under which we have to work are unfavorable. At EXPLO Campus Crusade leaders announced that in August each state would have Operation Penetration conferences to train those who couldn't attend EXPLO in evangelism and discipleship, and to give those who had attended EXPLO opportunities to plan ways to reach their state for Christ.

A 'Ridiculous' Plan

August is the worst time of the year to try to have a large meeting in the Phoenix area. It attracts mobs of winter tourists, but during the summer — especially in late July and August — just the opposite happens. Not only do the tourists stay away from the oppressive heat, but also every resident who can leave seeks a cooler climate. Those who can't become apathetic in the heat, avoiding almost all outdoor activity except swimming. Large gatherings in August are unheard of.

Even though conditions didn't look too promising, Elmer and our staff worked hard to plan Operation Penetration: we prayed that 900 would attend.

When Elmer and a staff member, Doug Broyles, went to a catering service to order food for the conference, the caterer just laughed at them. "What would ever bring that many people together?" he asked. "Don't you realize it's about 110° outside?"

Elmer wasn't discouraged. Instead he used it as an opportunity to witness, suggesting, "Doug, why don't you briefly tell our friend why we're doing what we're doing and how you came to find reality in Jesus Christ?" Then Doug shared his testimony.

The caterer wasn't the only one who was skeptical of our plan. But we trusted God to attract people to the conference despite the heat and despite the fact that many people would be out of town. We felt that all our efforts would be worthwhile if only one person met Christ. Well over 900 people attended our conference, and as a result, many became Christians. How we praised God! Later a girl who trusted Christ during the conference joined Campus Crusade staff.

No matter how hard he tried to destroy us, our enemy, the devil, just couldn't stop the movement of God's Spirit. Instead of dying, our ministry continued to grow. Once again, in 1971, we were faced with having more students in LTC than our room could hold. Our meeting room held 75; more than 150 came to LTC. For a while, we had two separate LTC meetings each week. But we saw this as only a temporary solution. Our staff women began to pray for a bigger meeting room.

My Dream House

At first we thought we'd enlarge the room we already

had. There was a vacant lot next door. We wrote the doctor who owned it, asking if he'd sell the land to us. Soon after this, he phoned, asking if we wanted to sell him our house instead. Of course, we turned down this offer. We didn't want to move; we just needed more space for our ministry. I felt let down and wondered why God had allowed this to happen. But we kept praying for more space.

There was a house on the corner of College Avenue and 15th Street that I passed every day on my way to campus. It was a beautiful ivy-covered, western-style home with a double lawn and a garden of red roses — just the kind of house I'd dreamed about. One day I noticed that it was for sale and thought, "Wouldn't it be great if we could have the Campus Crusade house here?"

A few days later one of our local board members, Elmer Bradley, phoned. "I've found a house near campus that's just perfect for the ministry," he said. "It's only two blocks from campus, and it's large. It has a building in back that could be remodeled into a meeting room for 200. At the price they're asking, it won't be for sale long." As he went on and on describing this house, I realized that he was talking about my dream home, and I got excited. He was enthused, too, and wanted Elmer, the board chairman, Perry Mehan and me to see it right away. Elmer and Perry didn't share Elmer Bradley's excitement about buying a new Campus Crusade house, but they went with him to look at it. As they looked at the house, their attitude changed quickly. Perry told Elmer, "We'd be crazy not to take this house — it's perfect."

A few days later the local board unanimously voted to buy my dream house and to sell the one we currently were living in.

Reaping Bountifully

We didn't even have to try to sell our house. The doctor who owned the lot next door bought it immediately. With the help of many friends, we moved into our new home that summer.

God's newest provision for the expansion of our minis-try confirmed once again a principle we were already

familiar with: He who sows sparingly reaps sparingly, and
he who sows bountifully reaps bountifully (II Corinthians
9:6). Although the Bible gives this principle in the context
of financial giving, we found that it was true of our ministry, too. Throughout the years we'd sown God's Word
through evangelism and discipleship. God continued to
give us an abundant harvest as more students became
Christians and grew in their faith.

Now we were seeing an even greater harvest as God
answered many times over our prayer for fruit *and* the
prayer Elmer had prayed in college: "Lord, I want to see
100 people go into full-time Christian work as a result of
my ministry."

Chapter 9

One Man Times 400

Through Elmer's personal ministry, as well as indirectly through his position as Campus Crusade area director for Arizona, he saw more than 400 men and women begin to serve God full time. Although many of them have joined Campus Crusade staff, both in America and overseas, many others have become pastors, Christian educational directors or church music directors and have taken over church positions. Still others have joined Christian organizations such as Wycliffe Bible Translators and Child Evangelism Fellowship.

Although we'd expected God to draw 100 into His service as a result of our ministry, we never dreamed that He would increase that number to 400!

Many have asked why we think God allowed us to see so much fruit. But we couldn't explain it; we could only praise God for producing it and for allowing us to be involved.

I think people have also responded to certain strengths that God built into Elmer's life. First, Elmer demonstrated a strong faith in a mighty God. Every year he trusted God to see more people become Christians through the Arizona ministry than the year before. He was never satisfied merely to repeat last year's results. "I believe God wants to do more," he often said. As people around him saw Elmer's faith, they wanted to trust God to do bigger things, too.

Second, Elmer knew where he was going and he knew how to encourage others to go with him. "Elmer was not only committed verbally to biblical priorities," says Don Orvis, professor of evangelism at Denver Conservative Baptist Theological Seminary, "but he also didn't deviate from them experientially." He set a consistent example that said, "Follow me as I follow Christ." And people did!

Vision, Faith and Courage

As Elmer encouraged individuals in their walk with Christ, he constantly talked about the needs of the campus, the nation and the world. According to David Hine, a former Campus Crusade staff member, "Elmer showed students the big picture, then gave them a piece of it that they could handle personally, such as reaching their campus for Christ. But he always challenged them to something that only the Lord could do, and that they could only do in the power of the Spirit. He asked them to have vision to see, faith to believe and courage to do."

Elmer's emphasis on encouraging Christians to involve themselves in a full-time ministry stemmed from Christ's command in Matthew 9:37,38: "Then He said to His disciples, 'The harvest is plentiful, but the workers are few. Therefore, beseech the Lord of the harvest to send out workers into His harvest.' "

We combined prayer for more full-time Christian workers with various forms of encouragement. This is an important part of the Campus Crusade ministry, as well as our personal goal. Our purpose was to win people to Christ, build disciples and send them out to minister.

Because of this emphasis, Elmer required his staff to join him in praying for and prompting students and laymen to labor in the spiritual harvest. Early in each school year he gave each Arizona staff member a blue prayer card. "As you begin to work with your disciples and pray for them," Elmer told the staff, "I want you to ask them what they think God has for their lives. Write down the names of 10 people on this card and pray regularly for them and their goals. Then make sure to keep the challenge before them."

Praying For Workers

The prayer card read, "Father, we pray urgently for more laborers in Your harvest. If it be Your will, we pray that You would move in the hearts of these 10 people to join us."

The staff also gave Elmer the names they had written on the card, and he prayed for them, too. Last year they prayed that, out of 400 students, at least 50 would join them. God honored that prayer; 56 headed in that direction.

We saw the evangelization of the Arizona campuses as a way to reach our goal of building disciples who would make Christian service their lifetime work. As we taught our students evangelism and discipleship in a campus setting, we also urged them to use the same principles to minister after graduation in their churches, neighborhoods and jobs.

Through various speakers, conferences, and weekend and summer-long evangelistic projects, we reminded our students that the majority of the world's people still needed to hear about Jesus Christ. From its beginning, Campus Crusade has had a slogan that I believe is still true: Win the campus to Christ today and win the world for Christ tomorrow. We discipled college students — tomorrow's leaders — so they could go to various parts of the globe and have ministries of evangelism and discipleship.

Reaching Small Towns

One way the Arizona ministry focused students' attention on needs off campus was through participating in town outreaches. Our first town outreach, in 1966, resulted from an invitation to bring some students to speak at a church youth group meeting in Casa Grande, a small town in southern Arizona.

We took 10 students and another staff member with us to Casa Grande one Sunday afternoon. When we got there, 50 teenagers were waiting for us, half of them non-Christians that the youth group members had brought. Some of our students shared their testimonies. Over dinner the staff and college students presented the Four Spiritual Laws to some of the young people. We asked others to read an evangelistic article in Campus Crusade's *Collegiate Challenge* magazine. Then we gave them an opportunity to invite Jesus Christ into their lives. After this, one speaker shared how to have assurance of salvation and another told the group how to be filled with the Holy Spirit.

The teenagers were very receptive; 12 indicated that they had become Christians. The youth group members thanked us for showing them how to share their faith in Christ.

Since God had blessed that small meeting, we made ourselves available to work with churches in other towns to train their members in evangelism and discipleship. The training included an evangelistic meeting and door-to-door witnessing. In this way we could give students a desire to reach communities, as well as help small churches that wanted training in how to reach their towns for Christ.

One student, Dave Wooster, who actively shared his faith on campus, also wanted to see his hometown, Lake Havasu City, saturated with the gospel. One summer Dave took the initiative to contact pastors in the resort town, offering their churches a chance to participate in a town outreach. The following spring he coordinated the project. I don't remember the results of the outreach, but it changed Dave's life. He gained such a strong concern for his community's spiritual health that he later became an associate pastor of a church there. Five years later, when we had another outreach in Lake Havasu City, Dave helped coordinate it once again. Even now he spends much of his time discipling families in his church.

Speaking at Conferences

In 1971, Elmer began to speak at conferences outside Arizona. Speaking at two conferences a year provided him with an opportunity to admonish thousands to help fulfill the Great Commission. Usually Elmer spoke five times at each conference, beginning with his testimony and an invitation to trust Christ. Then he talked on various aspects of discipleship, such as the importance of studying and memorizing the Scriptures, what a disciple is, and practical tips on moving men to action. He always ended with a message called "Here Am I, Send Me," his challenge to proclaim the kingdom of God full time.

We were astounded by the way God used this last talk in the lives of conferees. Every time Elmer gave this talk, more than two-thirds of those in the audience stood up, committing their lives to Christian service.

A year ago a young Hawaiian couple visited us. "You probably don't remember us," they said, "but we heard you speak at a Campus Crusade conference in January, 1973.

"I became a Christian the first night of the conference," the young man continued, "and by the end of the week we were standing with the others to say, 'Here am I, send me.' " Now, after they'd graduated from college, they were going to a South Seas island to minister spiritually and vocationally with The *Agape* Movement.

Although Elmer used conferences to recruit manpower for the Great Commission, he focused on individuals whom he personally encouraged and discipled.

A Magic Businessman

For example, Elmer met Bob Gurtler, a new Christian, at a Christian businessmen's breakfast in Phoenix. When he learned that Bob was a professional illusionist as well as a businessman, he promptly invited him to perform at an ASU student leaders' banquet. The banquet turned out to be more than a routine performance for Bob. As he listened to the testimonies of several students, he wanted to grow in his walk with God, too.

Elmer urged Bob to become a witness for Christ, and Bob attended LTC — Leadership Training Class — for training in evangelism and discipleship. When Bob mentioned that he was taking a week's vacation, Elmer asked him to spend six hours on two days of it with him, sharing his faith at ASU. Bob accepted Elmer's offer, and during those two days on campus, five of seven students they talked to trusted Christ.

"Six hours may not sound like much time," Bob said, "but God used those hours to change the entire course of my life."

The results of those hours thrilled Bob so much that he invented illusions to illustrate the gospel to use in his performances. He also taught an evangelistic Bible study for his real estate co-workers. Several months later Bob asked Elmer, "Do you think Campus Crusade could use an illusionist like me?"

Elmer and Bob discussed the possibility of Bob's joining Campus Crusade staff. "At that time, there were many people who were telling me that God could never use a magician: 'If you want to be all that God wants you to be, you'll have to give up magic, and go into the ministry or be a missionary,'" Bob recalled.

"In spite of the opposition," he continued, "Carl Heath, Elmer Lappen and Bill Bright were willing to risk their reputations to encourage me to serve Jesus Christ."

Bob — better known as André Kole — and his wife, Alice, joined Campus Crusade staff in 1963 as traveling representatives. Since then, he has performed before millions of students, military personnel and laymen all over the world. Thousands have come to know God after seeing his unique presentation of the gospel.

Bob readily attributes the success of his ministry to God's power. He's also grateful that Carl, Elmer and Bill recognized his potential at a time when others didn't. "I have always by nature been very shy and reserved," he said. "I was always terrified when anybody asked me to speak in public, and I flunked speech in college. Yet during the next years, God gave me the opportunity to share Christ with millions of people in 73 countries simply because these three men were willing to risk their reputations to love me and encourage me."

Illusions and Reality

In his shows, Bob does illusions that demonstrate the deceptiveness of the occult world — talking about spiritualism, witchcraft, communication with the dead, ESP and astrology. Then he encourages the audience to leave the world of illusion for the reality of a personal relationship with Jesus Christ.

During a three-month tour of Asia and the Middle East in 1973, Bob performed 100 times for more than 110,000 people in 13 countries (including Lebanon, Pakistan, India, Korea and Malaysia). In addition, he presented the gospel over national TV in five countries. Although most people in the audiences had previously heard little or nothing about Christ, more than 10,000 indicated that they had become Christians at Bob's programs. Local Campus Crusade staff, students and laymen personally followed up the new believers.

Another individual deeply affected by Elmer was Duane McDonough. Elmer met Duane on the ASU campus one afternoon as the student sat outside the business administration building holding a huge stack of books. "Hey, fella, are you trying to kid the world?" Elmer joked. "You know you won't study all those books."

Duane looked up, laughing. After they'd talked for a few minutes, Elmer asked if they could meet to get Duane's opinions on a collegiate religious survey. As it turned out, Duane was late for the appointment, but he was interested in a more personal religious faith.

Time ran out before Elmer could finish his presentation of the gospel, so he said, "I'm sorry, Duane. Right now I'm supposed to meet those two guys over there, and they want to know God, too. Can we get together here at the same time Thursday to finish our talk?"

When a person is interested, we usually finish sharing the gospel right then, even if we're late for our next appointment. Yet because Duane was genuinely interested, he agreed to meet Elmer again. Two days later he received Christ with Elmer.

Duane was so excited about his new faith that he brought two friends to his first follow-up appointment. They, too, trusted Christ. Duane began to develop a purpose in life that he'd lacked before. Instead of avoiding Christians, as he'd done previously, he spent time with them and studied the Bible. He also told others how they could become Christians.

'I Don't Believe It'

But a few months later Duane told Elmer, "I don't want to meet with you anymore. I don't believe in Christianity now."

Elmer was heartbroken — Duane was one of his key disciples! Feeling sick to his stomach, Elmer asked, "Why not?"

"I've been talking to one of my professors, and he doesn't believe it. Now I'm not so sure I do."

Although Duane tried to cut Christ out of his life, Elmer made a point of continuing their friendship. Often he took Duane out for meals, and they talked. Elmer and the pastor of Duane's church prayed together that Duane would renew his relationship with God.

This patient love seemed to make a difference. Two months later Duane began to involve himself in Christian activities again. His walk with God became an important part of his life. Now Duane devotes full time to helping people develop a relationship with God, as he serves as a pastor in Wisconsin.

Stan Gabriel, a graduate student at ASU, was unsure of his relationship with Christ when Elmer first met him. As they talked, Elmer shared with Stan how he could be sure he was a Christian. After that, Stan began to grow in his faith, involving himself in our ministry. At ASU Stan began to develop a deep love for God's Word and a desire to help people understand it.

That love of the Bible continued after graduation as Stan served as an officer in the Army. Elmer often wrote Stan, encouraging him to continue to study the Bible. When Stan came back from Vietnam, he showed us the New Testament we'd given him for graduation. Its cover was falling off, and the pages were worn. "Elmer, I've read this," Stan quipped.

Soon Stan joined Campus Crusade staff, taking assignments at ASU and in Utah. Later he taught both new and senior staff more about the Scriptures through Campus Crusade's Training Ministry. Now Stan and his wife, Ginger, have a ministry of evangelism and discipleship in Spain.

In March, 1978, they were assigned to Madrid to start lay, campus and Here's Life ministries. (Here's Life campaigns are city-wide evangelistic efforts in which churches band together to share the gospel with as many as possible in their city. New Christians are encouraged to attend follow-up Bible studies and involve themselves in local churches.) Stan spends most of his time contacting pastors and other Christian leaders, introducing them to Campus Crusade's ministry. He makes himself available to train and encourage those who want to learn more about the practical basics of the Christian life.

According to Stan, many pastors are discouraged in their ministries. A recent survey of European Christians showed that an estimated 50% of the Protestants are unsure of their salvation, 95% have no knowledge of the Holy Spirit and 98% do not share their faith in Christ regularly. tion, 95% have no knowledge of the Holy Spirit and 98% do not share their faith in Christ regularly.

To help meet these needs, Stan conducts seminars to train Spanish Christians in discipleship and evangelism, and how to follow up new believers. He also conducts management training seminars to help pastors and missionaries.

After a seminar on discipleship and evangelism, one pastor commented, "My church has experienced a spiritual renewal as a result of your seminar."

Stan has helped to form and lead a pastors' action group that prays, plans and ministers in preparation for Here's Life, World, to be held in the fall of 1980 or 1981. One of the pastors is now ready to lead the group himself. Stan also leads a Bible study on the Gospel of John for embassy personnel from four countries. Similar experiences have been repeated in the lives of over 400 men and women during our 23-year ministry — and God has done it all!

Ongrowing Ministry

After EXPLO '72 and Operation Penetration (the follow-up conference to EXPLO that offered evangelism and discipleship training, and discussion of ways to reach the state for Christ), our ministry throughout Arizona continued to grow. We were assigned an area administrator and an area secretary, to whom Elmer could delegate many of the ministry's financial and business tasks. But Elmer had to spend most of his time directing the state's campus, high school and lay ministries. This left little time for a personal ministry at ASU, although he still led a small discipleship group.

In August, 1977, Elmer anticipated an additional responsibility. Our ASU staff team had increased to 12 men and women, including us. This team was assigned to develop a larger ministry at ASU in preparation for a training center that Campus Crusade planned to begin there the following year. Elmer would direct this training center, and the ASU staff would train a group of new campus staff for ministries in other parts of the country.

Looking forward to a bigger and better ministry year, Elmer had planned an area staff meeting for Monday, August 15, but the staff had to meet without us. In a semicoma, Elmer struggled for his life at Desert Samaritan Hospital in Mesa.

Chapter 10

Fighting For Life

Sunday evening, August 14, was unusual in more ways than one. Elmer, Bev, Steve and I had gone to the evening service at our church, Grace Community Church of the Valley, as we usually did. Normally I parked the car near the sanctuary in a space reserved for handicapped people. But that night we got there a little late, and I had to park in a different area on the other side of the large church complex.

After church, Elmer and I talked to several friends, including a Campus Crusade staff couple from Africa who were in town for a short visit. By the time we'd finished our chat, most of the other people had already left. Bev and Steve had gone home with a friend, which was unusual.

Most of the lights had already been turned off, so it was dark as I briskly pushed Elmer's wheelchair into the parking lot. Suddenly the wheels hit a drainage dip in the pavement that I hadn't seen. I lost control of the chair as it fell to the right, throwing Elmer out. Running around the overturned chair, I tried to catch Elmer, but couldn't reach him fast enough. Watching him fall and not being able to prevent it gave me the most helpless feeling I've ever had.

Getting Help

Elmer was thrown underneath a car, gashing his right temple and landing hard on his knees. When I saw his head starting to bleed, I ran to get help into a building where a youth meeting was taking place. "Come help me quick!" I blurted out to the first person I saw. "Elmer just fell out of his wheelchair!"

Several people ran back to the parking lot with me, and soon 15 people had gathered. The Rev. Guy Davidson, the senior pastor, called an ambulance. Paramedics, police and an ambulance came immediately, sirens blaring. The paramedics put Elmer on a stretcher, and the ambulance rushed him to the nearest hospital.

Pastor Davidson and Pastor Jim Rentz and their families went with me to the hospital, which was only a couple of miles from the church. The doctor quickly stitched up Elmer's head and ordered X-rays.

The X-rays didn't show any evidence of a concussion, and the doctor didn't think Elmer was injured seriously, since the gash on his head wasn't deep. According to routine, he put Elmer in another room for observation.

I phoned the children and told them about the accident; they went to bed, thinking everything was fine.

Shock and Painful Knees

About midnight, Elmer went into shock. The doctors treated him for it and kept watching him. He began to complain that his knees hurt. We thought that the accident had caused his arthritis to flare up.

Soon Elmer wasn't very rational. It seemed like the nurses were asking Elmer and me 10,000 questions about his medical history and that of his family. In answer to one question, Elmer mentioned that his mother was alive, but both his parents were dead.

Soon Dr. Victor Sartor, who had been assigned to Elmer's case, came in and took charge. Slowly Elmer began to pull out of shock. About 3 a.m. on Monday, Dr. Sartor told me that Elmer needed to stay in intensive care so the nurses could keep an eye on him the rest of the night. Pastor Rentz drove me home.

About 9 that morning, a nurse phoned, asking me about Elmer's sleep habits. She told me that he was in a semicoma and that the nurses couldn't wake him up. Alarmed, I got ready to go to the hospital.

Before I left, I saw Bill Wilson, our ASU senior staff man, when he came to our house for the staff meeting. "You'll have to take over the staff meeting this morning," I said, explaining what had happened to Elmer.

A Puzzling Condition

When I got to the hospital, the doctors were giving Elmer various tests. They were puzzled because, normally, a head injury would have caused his lack of consciousness. Yet there had been no sign of a concussion, and they didn't know what was causing this semicoma. Earlier in the morning, Elmer's temperature and heartbeat had changed. He woke up for a few seconds, staring blankly. He didn't recognize anyone and couldn't speak. When he was moved, he groaned in pain.

Finally, the doctors reached the conclusion that Elmer had had a heart attack during the night. Apparently it had injured the brain stem, which controls speech, consciousness and motor control.

I don't know all the tests that Elmer had; I couldn't follow the medical terminology. But I prayed, knowing that he was in pain with his arthritis. I wasn't fearful, because right after the accident God had given me peace that He was in control of Elmer's condition. Also, Pastor Davison, Pastor Rentz, their wives and other members of the large Grace Community Church stayed with me in the waiting room. There was someone with me constantly that week, and their presence and love for us encouraged me.

During the tests, Elmer suddenly stopped breathing. The hospital staff rushed him back to his room and put him under an oxygen mask. He remained under it until the next day, with a heart monitor also attached to his chest. It was on Monday afternoon that Hal Jones and I prayed in Elmer's hospital room, as I mentioned in Chapter 1, noting that Elmer's heart beat for God and asking God to heal him.

Not Expected to Live

I didn't know this until later, but Dr. Sartor didn't expect Elmer to live through Monday night. He even told his associate, who took over for him late that night, "Don't be surprised if Elmer isn't with us tomorrow."

Early Tuesday morning, while we waited at the hospital, Pastor Rentz suggested, "Maybe we should have a special prayer meeting for Elmer. Are you familiar with the passage in James 5:14,15 that talks about the church elders anointing a sick person with oil and praying for him? I think you should pray about doing this."

"I don't have to pray about it," I answered immediately.
"I think we should definitely plan to do it."

"Okay," Pastor Rentz said, "what about Wednesday
night after church? That will give you time to get some
people together. Start praying about who should be there."

I asked him to participate, since he believed that God
would honor this type of prayer meeting, and he agreed to
come.

That afternoon, Elmer was able to breathe without the
oxygen mask, so it was removed. Otherwise, there was no
change in his health for the next three days. Because of his
arthritis, the hospital staff frequently had to turn him
over in bed, and this caused Elmer great pain. Since he
couldn't eat, he was being fed intravenously.

Sometime Tuesday Jon phoned long distance. He was
on a trip to Alaska, and I hadn't known where to contact
him. I told him about Elmer, and we made arrangements
for him to fly home the next day.

Prayer for Healing

Then I planned the prayer meeting, which we'd decided to have at 10 Wednesday night. Pastor Rentz explained to Dr. Sartor what we wanted to do and got his
permission to have the meeting. Pastor Rentz and I had
decided that six people should participate, and I prayed
about four others to invite. Finally I chose friends who had
strong faith — Hal Jones; Wayne Shuart, a layman from
Phoenix; Bobbie Taylor, my long-time prayer partner; and
Bob Glab, another pastor at Grace Community Church.
Each one promised to join Pastor Rentz and me at the
meeting.

Sixteen-year-old Bev and 13-year-old Steve listened as
I invited people to the prayer meeting. They knew that the
ASU staff had also asked people all over the country to
pray during the meeting. They had been afraid to visit
Elmer before. But as they heard me plan the meeting, they
sensed my anticipation of what God would do, and they
asked me if they could come, too. I was thrilled that they
wanted to participate and immediately gave them permission to join us.

When Jon arrived Wednesday afternoon, he went to visit Elmer. He was stunned to see his dad in a semicoma. When he found out about the prayer meeting, he asked to come with us.

The nine of us gathered at 9 p.m. and went to the hospital chapel to pray and discuss the meeting. Later, standing around Elmer's bed, each of us read a prayer promise and prayed conversationally. The verse I claimed was Jeremiah 33:3: "Call to Me, and I will answer you, and I will tell you great and mighty things, which you do not know."

I don't remember what everyone prayed during the 45-minute meeting, but Jon's prayer made an impact on me. He prayed, "Lord, we don't demand that You do anything here, but I'd like to see Dad talk. Even if You don't do anything, we'll just thank You."

We all sensed God's presence in a special way. Pastor Rentz anointed Elmer with oil, and the group sang several hymns. Elmer was aware that something was happening, but he still didn't recognize us and was only semiconscious. We saw a fast answer to Jon's prayer when, near the end of the meeting, Elmer sang a favorite hymn, "Only Believe," with us! We were relieved to hear Elmer's gravelly voice again!

No Change

Thursday morning I looked forward to visiting Elmer. We'd had such an exciting prayer meeting the night before, and I expected God to start healing him. But when I got to the hospital, I found that Elmer was no better. He still didn't know who I was, although he could tell that someone was there. NO change! That afternoon I went home and cried in disappointment.

The next morning when I went to see Elmer, he was awake. He looked at me and recognized me! How I praised God that He'd answered our prayers after all! "What happened?" Elmer asked.

I explained about the fall; at first he didn't remember it, but later he recalled what had happened. Elmer didn't remember being admitted to the hospital or anything that had happened that week.

That day, Elmer was a little confused, but he gradually became able to think and understand again. The doctor kept asking him questions like, "What year is this?" and "Who's the President of the United States?" to see how much he could think and communicate.

He didn't talk much at first, but he improved rapidly. He was rational and able to eat. Dr. Sartor and the rest of the hospital staff were amazed with Elmer's quick come-back, although Elmer still was attached to the heart monitor. On Monday morning, they transferred him to an intermediate care unit. By Tuesday, as he continued to get better, he was taken to a regular hospital room.

The doctor was afraid Elmer's arthritic joints would lose their ability to move, so he told the nurses to get him up out of bed occasionally. When they tried to set Elmer in a chair, the movement hurt him so much that he screamed. He also kept complaining that his knees hurt. Finally I asked Dr. Sartor, "What are you going to do about Elmer's knees? He's having more pain than usual; maybe there's something wrong."

Dr. Sartor ordered X-rays, and they showed that Elmer's right knee was broken and that his left knee was cracked. The doctors put casts on both legs.

A Miraculous Recovery

During his recuperation, Elmer was overwhelmed to see the number of friends he had all over the world. He'd never realized before the number of people he'd met and grown close to throughout his ministry. However, the many telegrams, letters, phone calls, flowers and prayers he received while he was recovering convinced him of their love for him. Many staff, students, and members of our church came to encourage him while he was in the hospital and later when he came home.

As usual, Elmer took advantage of his contact with the doctors and the nurses to share his faith with them. More than once Dr. Sartor told him, "Your recovery is a miracle. I didn't expect you to live through the Monday night after your accident. The Man Upstairs must have more for you to do."

Elmer quickly answered, "Dr. Sartor, I believe that Man to be Jesus Christ."

One nurse, Jean, organized Elmer's care into a daily routine, which he welcomed. As she spent time feeding him or, with others' help, turning him over in bed, he told her about Jesus Christ. He also gave her a printed copy of his testimony. Jean didn't trust Christ then, but she did so later as another nurse continued to witness to her.

Elmer was discharged from the hospital one month after his accident. Although he didn't need constant care, his casts were so heavy I couldn't move him alone. And I'd have to move him several times a day. Because of this, I made arrangements to transfer Elmer to a local nursing home until his casts were removed.

After Elmer had been in the nursing home approximately two weeks, Pastor Rentz asked him, "Elmer, how long will you be in those casts?"

"The doctor said I'd have to keep them on for 28 more days."

"Oh, that's too long," the pastor objected. "Let's pray that the Lord gets you out of them in 14 days." Then they prayed about it together.

Eleven days later Elmer's casts were taken off. Now he could come home! The orthopedic doctor had thought Elmer's fractures might not mend properly because of his arthritis. But the last time Elmer went to him, the doctor practically danced around the room. He couldn't believe how well the bones had healed.

We Didn't Know Why

When I took Elmer home on October 9, he was very weak and had to spend the next two and a half months regaining his strength. But our prayers had been answered! Even though he wasn't strong enough to participate in as many activities as he had before the heart attack, he eventually resumed his ministry.

Many people asked us why we thought God allowed Elmer to experience this accident and the physical problems that followed it. Each time we had to answer that we didn't know. One of Elmer's favorite sayings was, "You can trust God, even when you can't trace Him." We certainly couldn't trace God's purpose in these physical problems.

Yet Elmer and I believed that God was in control, and we trusted Him. Even though this situation looked like a tragedy at first, the result was that God was glorified. He showed Himself strong to those who had prayed by healing Elmer in answer to our prayers. Also, the whole chain of events was a witness to many doctors and nurses who may not have been Christians.

One lesson Elmer learned was a fresh appreciation for the power of prayer. "I've always had a faith barrier that prayers of healing wouldn't work for me," he admitted. "But on August 17 those prayers did work, and I'm excited about the future because that answer to prayer might be the beginning of many more."

Elmer was also reminded of the brevity of life. When Dr. Sartor told him that he'd almost died on August 15, he was more willing to slow down and take time to recover fully. Before then, Elmer would have never considered cutting down his involvement in ministry activities. Although Elmer was still very weak and saw the wisdom of resting, he didn't enjoy sitting on the sidelines. His heart was out on campus with the rest of the staff.

Being reminded of the shortness of life also gave Elmer an assurance that he was indeed pouring his life into the things that would matter most in eternity: his close relationship with God and helping others to develop the same kind of walk. Because of this assurance, Elmer could return to the same type of ministry he'd had before, knowing that he was accomplishing exactly what God had called him to do.

Chapter 11

Homecoming

After four months of recuperation from his heart attack and accident, Elmer gradually resumed his responsibilities as Arizona area director and ASU campus director. Although he never totally regained his strength, he poured all he had into his ministry, rarely doing anything else.

Nineteen months later, on March 25, 1979, Elmer suddenly went to be with the Lord.

We spent the week of March 11-16 at a Campus Crusade directors' conference in Williamsburg, Va. There several people, including Elmer, got sick with a virus. Elmer stayed in bed Thursday and Friday, and I went to the rest of the meetings, coming back often to check on him.

When it was time to go home on Saturday, Elmer was well enough to make the exhausting 14-hour car and plane trip. The next day he rested and prepared for the monthly Arizona staff meeting on Monday.

Although Elmer was still sick, he went to the staff meeting, which normally lasted most of the day. An hour before lunch break, he asked to leave the meeting, saying that he would return later. But Elmer was too sick to go back to the meeting.

He spent much of that week resting. But he also did things that had to be done immediately, such as finishing important area paperwork and directing the ASU staff meeting Wednesday afternoon.

On Friday, I took him to Dr. Sartor because I thought his illness was lasting longer than it should. The doctor discovered that Elmer had pneumonia, although he didn't think Elmer was ill enough to be hospitalized.

Elmer Gets Weaker

Two days later, on Sunday, I noticed that Elmer was much weaker. I phoned the doctor, describing Elmer's condition, and he told me to bring him to the hospital immediately. Since he was too weak to ride in the car, I called an ambulance.

Elmer kept getting weaker. When the ambulance arrived, the attendants said he was going into shock, gave him oxygen and rushed him to the hospital emergency room. Elmer was admitted to the coronary care unit, since he'd previously had a heart attack. Although he was being treated for pneumonia, the doctor watched for possible heart problems.

Elmer continued to get worse quickly and was suffering much pain. His kidneys failed, and a specialist began to try various things. I went in and out of Elmer's room several times that afternoon, staying with him as long as the doctors would let me. Unlike his previous hospital stay, Elmer was conscious of everything that was happening.

I phoned my best friend, Bobbie Taylor, and asked her to call our church's prayer chain about Elmer. I also called our children, Bev and Steve, asking them to bring me something for lunch. After I ate, I drove them home so I could keep the car. Almost as soon as we got home, about 4 p.m., the doctor phoned to tell me that Elmer's illness was very serious. Until then, things were happening so fast that I hadn't realized that Elmer was facing death. Immediately I went back to the hospital.

As the news spread, several people came to visit me briefly at the hospital. During our church's evening service, the entire congregation — close to 1,000 people, I was told — had prayed for Elmer. About 9:30, Elmer began to gasp for air, and I ran for the nurse. She came back with me, gave an emergency call and asked me to leave the room. Eight doctors and nurses ran into Elmer's room, and I knew that he was dying.

'Take Elmer Quickly'

The only person in the hall besides me was an ASU staff member, Craig Colle. We just sat there looking at each other, unable to talk because of emotions. I prayed silently, "Lord, it's all right with me if You take Elmer to be with You quickly. You don't have to prolong his suffering for my sake. He's already been through so much pain! I'd be happier if he didn't have to suffer any more."

About 20 minutes later, Elmer died of a massive heart attack.

Although it was painful for me to lose my beloved husband, God immediately flooded me with His peace about Elmer's death.

When Elmer had his first heart attack, I'd felt strongly that we should fight it. I believed his work wasn't finished yet and that we needed to trust God to heal him.

After the second heart attack, God gave me assurance that it was His perfect will for Elmer to die then. He'd finished his work as a director; since Elmer had just told each staff member what his responsibilities were, the staff could keep the ministry going for the rest of the semester without Elmer. God had also recently granted to Elmer the things he would have wanted most if he'd known he was going to die soon: an active, fruitful ministry until the end; a visit with Jon in Washington, D.C. (where he served in the Navy); a visit with his brother, Sam; and an opportunity to speak about Christ to 400 men at church in which 17 received Christ. God had allowed Elmer to experience fully the truth of his life verse: "You have let me experience the joys of life and the exquisite pleasures of Your own eternal presence" (Psalm 16:11, Living Bible).

A New Body

Too, Elmer looked forward to going to be physically with the Lord. Because his earthly body gave him so much pain, he could hardly wait to get the new, perfect body that Jesus promises every believer. This promise was reality to him, not just a passage he'd read in Scripture. In fact, Elmer often quoted Philippians 3:20,21, "But our homeland is in heaven, where our Savior the Lord Jesus Christ is; and we are looking forward to His return from there. When He comes back He will take these dying bodies of ours and change them into glorious bodies like His own, using the same mighty power that He will use to conquer all else everywhere" (LB).

God also assured me that "His loved ones are very precious to Him and He does not lightly let them die" (Psalm 116:15, LB). God had graciously prepared us in every way for Elmer's death. Not only had He allowed Elmer to finish his work and given him his strongest desires, but He had also prepared me to live and minister without Elmer.

After Elmer died, there was no question about my staying on Campus Crusade staff. Our call to this ministry was always my call, too, not just Elmer's. And I believed that God wanted me to keep serving Him through Campus Crusade. Even though I hadn't had the opportunity to have a full-time ministry of evangelism and discipleship for many years, I had the necessary training and experience to start one.

God gave Pastor Davidson and me wisdom as we planned Elmer's funeral service. We wanted it to honor the Lord, to let people know about Elmer's commitment and ministry, and to be a joyful occasion that showed our faith that Elmer was alive in heaven.

Praise and Worship

We held the memorial service the following Thursday, March 29, at Grace Community Church. Approximately 1,000 Campus Crusade staff, students and laymen attended the praise and worship service. The group listened intently, reverently expectant that this funeral wouldn't be gloomy.

The four-man chain that Elmer had often used as an example of spiritual multiplication shared their testimonies and memories of how God had used Elmer in their lives. All four have developed dynamic ministries of their own — Bob Gurtler and Doug Broyles as Campus Crusade staff members, Don Orvis as a seminary professor of evangelism, and Carl Heath as a layman.

They and the other two speakers, Pastor Davidson and Bill Bright, encouraged their listeners to commit themselves to God with the same whole-heartedness that Elmer had had. The focus was on God, and that's just what Elmer would have wanted.

In closing the service, Bill urged everyone to share the Four Spiritual Laws with at least one person within the next 24 hours. Then he prayed that at least 1,000 people would become Christians during that time, to glorify God and as a memorial to Elmer. I don't know how many actually did so, but many told me later that day that they intended to witness to someone before the end of the next day.

I think Bob Gurtler best summed up the message that God wanted to communicate through Elmer's life: "When Jesus set out to change the world, He didn't choose the most likely candidates, but He chose a very unlikely group of men," Bob said. "I think God takes great delight in using what the world says is unusable. And God used Elmer Lappen in a way that few people have ever been used before.

"Many people were praying for Elmer's healing," Bob continued, "and I think it's important to know that God heals all of His children — sometimes in this life, sometimes in the life to come. The reason, I believe, that God didn't heal Elmer in this life is that He had a far greater lesson to demonstrate to each one of us. I think the thing God wants us to know through the life of Elmer Lappen is this fact: If He could use Elmer Lappen to do what he did — with the limitations and the suffering that he went through — then He can use you and me if we're simply willing to be totally committed to Him."

> "I have fought the good fight, I have finished the course, I have kept the faith; in the future there is laid up for me the crown of righteousness, which the Lord, the righteous Judge, will award to me on that day; and not only to me, but also to all who have loved His appearing"
>
> (II Timothy 4:7,8).

Have You Heard of the Four Spiritual Laws?

Just as there are physical laws that govern the physical universe, so are there spiritual laws which govern your relationship with God.

LAW ONE

GOD **LOVES** YOU, AND OFFERS A WONDERFUL **PLAN** FOR YOUR LIFE.

(References should be read in context from the Bible wherever possible.)

God's Love

"For God so loved the world, that He gave His only begotten Son, that whoever believes in Him should not perish, but have eternal life" (John 3:16).

God's Plan

(Christ speaking) "I came that they might have life, and might have it abundantly" (that it might be full and meaningful) (John 10:10).

Why is it that most people are not experiencing the abundant life?

Because . . .

LAW TWO

MAN IS **SINFUL** and **SEPARATED** FROM GOD. THEREFORE, HE CANNOT KNOW AND EXPERIENCE GOD'S LOVE AND PLAN FOR HIS LIFE.

Man Is Sinful

"For all have sinned and fall short of the glory of God" (Romans 3:23).

Man was created to have fellowship with God; but, because of his stubborn self-will, he chose to go his own independent way and fellowship with God was broken. This self-will, characterized by an attitude of active rebellion or passive indifference, is evidence of what the Bible calls sin.

111

Man Is Separated

"For the wages of sin is death" (spiritual separation from God) (Romans 6:23).

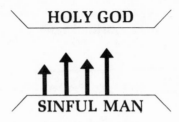

This diagram illustrates that God is holy and man is sinful. A great gulf separates the two. The arrows illustrate that man is continually trying to reach God and the abundant life through his own efforts, such as a good life, philosophy or religion.

The third law explains the only way to bridge this gulf . . .

LAW THREE

JESUS CHRIST IS GOD'S **ONLY** PROVISION FOR MAN'S SIN. THROUGH HIM YOU CAN KNOW AND EXPERIENCE GOD'S LOVE AND PLAN FOR YOUR LIFE.

He Died in Our Place

"But God demonstrates His own love toward us, in that while we were yet sinners, Christ died for us" (Romans 5:8).

He Rose from the Dead

"Christ died for our sins . . . He was buried . . . He was raised on the third day, according to the Scriptures . . . He appeared to Peter, then to the twelve. After that He appeared to more than five hundred . . ." (I Corinthians 15:3-6).

He Is the Only Way to God

"Jesus said to him, 'I am the way, and the truth, and the life; no one comes to the Father, but through Me' " (John 14:6).

112

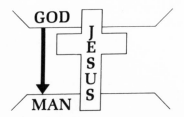

This diagram illustrates that God has bridged the gulf which separates us from God by sending His Son, Jesus Christ, to die on the cross in our place to pay the penalty for our sins.

It is not enough just to know these three laws . . .

LAW FOUR

WE MUST INDIVIDUALLY **RECEIVE** JESUS CHRIST AS SAVIOR AND LORD; THEN WE CAN KNOW AND EXPERIENCE GOD'S LOVE AND PLAN FOR OUR LIVES.

We Must Receive Christ

"But as many as received Him, to them He gave the right to become children of God, even to those who believe in His name" (John 1:12).

We Receive Christ through Faith

"For by grace you have been saved through faith; and that not of yourselves, it is the gift of God; not as a result of works, that no one should boast" (Ephesians 2:8,9).

When We Receive Christ, We Experience a New Birth

(Read John 3:1-8).

We Receive Christ by Personal Invitation

(Christ is speaking) "Behold, I stand at the door and knock; if any one hears My voice and opens the door, I will come in to him" (Revelation 3:20).

Receiving Christ involves turning from self to God (repentance) and trusting Christ to come into our lives to forgive our sins and to make us the kind of person He wants us to be. Just to agree intellectually that Jesus Christ is the Son of God and that He died on the cross for our sins is not enough. Nor is it enough to have an emotional experience. We receive Jesus Christ by faith, as an act of the will.

These two circles represent two kinds of lives:

SELF-DIRECTED LIFE
S—Self on the throne
†—Christ is outside the life
•—Interests are directed by self, often resulting in discord and frustration

CHRIST-DIRECTED LIFE
†—Christ is in the life
S—Self is yielding to Christ
•—Interests are directed by Christ, resulting in harmony with God's plan

Which circle best represents your life?

Which circle would you like to have represent your life?

The following explains how you can receive Christ:

YOU CAN RECEIVE CHRIST RIGHT NOW BY FAITH THROUGH PRAYER

(Prayer is talking with God)

God knows your heart and is not so concerned with your words as He is with the attitude of your heart. The following is a suggested prayer:

"Lord Jesus, I need You. Thank You for dying on the cross for my sins. I open the door of my life and receive You as my Savior and Lord. Thank You for forgiving my sins and giving me eternal life. Make me the kind of person You want me to be."

Does this prayer express the desire of your heart?

If it does, pray this prayer right now, and Christ will come into your life, as He promised.